HOW
ORGANIZATIONS
ARE REPRESENTED
IN
WASHINGTON

THE BOBBS-MERRILL COMPANY, INC.

INDIANAPOLIS AND NEW YORK

HOW ORGANIZATIONS ARE REPRESENTED IN WASHINGTON

Lewis Anthony Dexter

DEDICATION
AND ACKNOWLEDGMENTS

Five people created and stimulated my interest in problems of Washington representation and government relations. To two of them, and to the memory of the other three, this book is dedicated:

My mother, Elisabeth Anthony Dexter, formerly an officer of the American Association of University Women and the Women's International League for Peace and Freedom, and a student of the woman's rights' movement.

My faculty adviser in graduate school, E. Pendleton Herring, author of the first two modern, general studies in this field, *Public Administration and the Public Interest* (McGraw-Hill, 1936) and *Group Representation Before Congress* (Johns Hopkins, 1929),[1] now President of the Social Science Research Council.

My grandfather, Alfred Williams Anthony, a founder of the National Conference of Christians and Jews, active on many committees of the then Federal Council of Churches, Executive Secretary of the Home Missions Council, etc. (died 1939).

My father, Robert C. Dexter, Director of the Department of Social Relations, American Unitarian Association, 1927–1941, later active in refugee relief work and refugee legislation, and then Chairman, Executive Committee, World Federation of United Nations Associations (died 1955).

My first and most vigorous sponsor, Henry A. Atkinson, General Secretary for a quarter of a century of the Church Peace

---

[1] Both these books were reissued by Russell and Russell in 1967.

Union and one of the organizers of the League to Enforce
Peace (died 1960).

Anyone who reads this book will see how much it has been
shaped and organized by my collaboration with Raymond A.
Bauer and Ithiel de Sola Pool in our joint *American Business
and Public Policy** (Atherton, 1963): my obligation to them is
great. I also profited much from the stimulus to think about
these problems provided by my colleagues in the year 1952, Bertram M. Gross, author of *The Legislative Struggle* (McGraw-Hill,
1953) and Jerome Spingarn, himself formerly a Washington
representative. I am also grateful to Mr. Spingarn for suggesting,
specifically, one of the major themes in Chapter Eight.

It is perhaps appropriate to mention also that everything I
have ever written has, in one way or another, been influenced by
three outstanding teachers, Carl J. Friedrich of Harvard University, Earl S. Johnson, formerly of the University of Chicago and
now at the University of Wisconsin, Milwaukee, and the late
Charles E. Merriam.

As far as recollection serves after nine years, the arrangement
that led to what became the first draft of this book was recom-
mended by William Brubeck, Boyd France, Michael Marsh, and
Meyer Rashish. In any event, I am indebted to each one of them
for ideas on these and related issues.

Above all, of course, my sense of obligation and gratitude go
out to the several thousand business executives, Washington
representatives, directors of government relations programs, congressmen, committee clerks, journalists, and government officials,
who, over the last thirty years, have taken time to be interviewed
by me and have explained to me how they dealt with government
relations problems. Some of them stand out very vividly in my

---

* I am grateful to Atherton Press, holders of the copyright for *American
Business and Public Policy*, for permission to use several paragraphs from
that book.

memory as especially helpful—for example, several officers of meat-packing firms in Chicago in 1943, and the late Senator Green of Rhode Island in 1953—but it would be indiscreet and invidious to make any extensive list. Some interviewees who are still active would not wish to be named.

In order to protect the confidence of these men, I have followed our practice in *American Business and Public Policy*. Examples are, of course, given, based upon interviews; but, to prevent embarrassing identification of individual respondents or organizations, peripheral details have been disguised or answers given in two different but similar interviews combined, etc. Therefore, also, the use of such invented names as "New Zanzuel," "Senator Personal Service," and the like.

Needless to say—but in the tradition of preface-writing nevertheless necessary to say—no one here mentioned has any responsibility for weaknesses, errors, and defects in the book. These are all of my own making.

LEWIS ANTHONY DEXTER

Belmont, Massachusetts
February 1968

CONTENTS

1

IT IS NOT JUST LOBBYING: GOVERNMENT RELATIONS AND WASHINGTON REPRESENTATION

What This Book Is About
and Whom It Is For

I.

The title of this chapter means what it says. "Washington representatives"—those who represent business firms, trade associations, state governments, trade unions, churches, recreational groups, professional organizations, chambers of commerce—are usually called "lobbyists." But their job—the job of government relations—is not *only* lobbying. In many cases, it is not *chiefly* lobbying. Many Washington representatives *never* have lobbied.

1. Anyone active in an organization that has a Washington representative (and that includes many readers of this book; see chapter two) can profit from discussion of what government rela-

tions really is like. Businessmen, association officials, state government administrators, and all executives directly responsible for a government relations program can benefit from analysis of the job. Most clients and employers of Washington representatives get far less advantage and service from them than they should because there is no general, coherent picture of what they can and cannot do.

2. Students of American government need to understand the Washington representative and his place in politics. This is of far more theoretical *and* practical importance for the beginning student or interested citizen than attempts to understand such matters as "the American party system."[1] *Washington representatives engage in a really new kind of representation.* They permit big government in a diversified society to adapt, to communicate, to coordinate. Vice versa, these men and women make it easier for particular groups to be heard, to communicate, to adjust.

3. *Washington representatives themselves need more professional self-confidence.* They should realize that in fact they are making a serious, professional contribution. Perhaps few of them will learn much new about techniques from this book. But many of them with whom I have talked seem to lack that high professional self-confidence which lawyers and doctors and public-health specialists have. When they begin to realize that many

[1] Which is simply a catalog of exceptions. I have nothing against attempts to understand it, whatever it may be—but after pointing out that it 1. differs among each of the fifty states, and 2. often differs within them (contrast Chicago and Joliet in 1956, or Watertown and Boston at that time, or Geneva and Auburn in 1948, or St. Petersburg and Tampa in 1964) and 3. is not a system but a peculiar mixture of local traditions and state election laws, an irrelevant European vocabulary and mass media simplifications, I, as a teacher of government, have nothing to say on the topic, whereas there is a good deal students and citizens can profitably learn about Washington representation. (For technically minded political scientists at an advanced level attempts to make sense out of the U.S. party system are weirdly fascinating; but they are not worth inflicting on interested citizens or students.) The party system is, of course, merely an example.

problems are common to the whole profession—and when they see the endemic dilemma of a professional role versus a service function, and choose the former—they will in the long run serve themselves, their clients, and society better. A profession based on the collective traditions, wisdom, and ethics of colleagues serves client needs, sometimes despite client preferences and demands. This attitude in law and medicine has proved to be of public utility. If Washington representatives were more thoroughly conscious of their professional character, they would find it easier to defend themselves against unreasonable demands by clients or employers.[2]

4. And, if this book were read by officials in the numerous governmental agencies which deal with Washington representatives, it might be of some value there, too. In a recent discussion with a selected group of career government officials, I was disappointed to note that some of them had no clear conception of what Washington representatives do. Yet many of these men have to deal frequently with representatives of business or labor or state government, etc. And to the degree that they are not aware of what the latter do, then they may not know as well as possible how to judge what is said, what is not said, what is priority, whom else to consult, etc.

5. Finally, as far as possible, it would be desirable if journalists and columnists appreciated the real job of Washington representatives. The general conception of lobbying is strongly reinforced, perhaps was created, by the emphases of the newspaper press. Newspapers must dramatize, show heroes and villains, and follow a simple story line. This may be due partly to the demands of readers, but in some measure it is because of the

---

[2] There are still two other ways of looking at the book: first, most of what it says, if worthwhile at all, applies to *anyone engaged in any sort of* "*government relations,*" whether or not with Washington; second, sociologists interested in "sociology of the professions" may find the picture enlarges *understanding of the free professions.*

scheduling and production processes of the newspaper industry.[3] In fact, this book—like many other *books*—is an effort to modify and correct a dramatic picture built up over years by newspaper exposés and newspaper columns—and, in this case, by newspaper use of congressional materials.

Congressional hearings on lobbying—and attacks by congressmen on lobbyists—are designed either to capture headlines and/or to show the "evil" character of opponents of measures which the attacking congressmen favor. There is no reason why congressmen should not seek such publicity; Congress is no forum for analytic studies of politics, for trying to describe objectively how things really happen. The findings of many congressional committees are essentially weapons in an ongoing battle. But if the press were to clarify and enlighten, it would not simply take such attacks and investigations at face value.

II.

It is evidently desirable to define "lobbying." According to the second edition of Merriam-Webster, "to lobby" means "to address or solicit members of a legislative body"—in this case, the United States Congress—"in the lobby or elsewhere with intent to influence legislation," and then, by derivation, "to urge or procure passage of [legislation] by lobbying." Presumably, although the dictionary does not say so explicitly, lobbying would include efforts to solicit members of Congress about nonlegislative matters over which they have control—such as appropriations, appointments to the military academies, investigations of essentially nonlegislative issues, confirmation of judicial appointments, etc.

---

[3] See W. Lloyd Warner, "The World of Biggy Muldoon: Transformation of a Political Hero," in L. Dexter and D. White, *People, Society, and Mass Communications* (New York: Free Press, 1964), pp. 337–358, for a relevant picture of the press and its interpretations of politics.

Originally, the word "lobbying" arose from the fact (still true in some state legislatures and foreign parliaments) that the easiest way to get hold of legislators was physically in the lobbies.[4] Nowadays members have offices and staff assistants, and other ways of communicating with them often prove more effective. For instance, a congressman may be invited to be a major speaker at an association meeting. The association staff will draft his speech for him, and he will give its ideas more attention because of what he is supposed to say. At the meeting, of course, he will talk directly with the leaders of the industry.

In general, the idea of "lobbying"—Washington representation—has acquired a discreditable meaning. In theory, it is nothing more than a special, intensive exercise of the right of petition; in practice it probably contributes a good deal, cumulatively, to social order and adaptation. Nevertheless, the notion that Washington representatives and lobbyists mostly bribe or threaten is widespread. For instance, a friend of mine, who used himself to work for a lobbying organization, asked his eight-year-old son at the dinner table what he thought my present book would be about. "Oh, I know," said the boy, "it's about things like how somebody pays somebody $3,000 to vote for a law and that sort of thing!"

Naturally, bribes and threats are among the weapons of political action; occasionally they are the only way to achieve political objectives. Certainly there have been Washington representatives who bribed or threatened. But they are quite exceptional—nearly as exceptional as the attorney who engages in clearly illegitimate tactics to win a case. There are—rarely—times when a Washington representative may or must point out to a client that, in fact,

---

[4] I do not believe any United States student of Washington lobbying has pointed out another way in which the architecture of lobbies created a verb. In Buenos Aires slang, "lobbear" used to mean "to sit around in hotel lobbies and eye the pretty girls." The word "lobby-sitting" has occasionally been used similarly in the United States.

under a particular set of circumstances, bribes or threats may be the way for the client to achieve his objectives. A Washington representative might, under some circumstances, inform clients who is supposed to be susceptible to what sort of bribe or threat. In fact, I myself once in a report for a client explained that an influential member of a relevant committee (now no longer in the Congress) might best be influenced by putting some of his law associates on a retainer. It should be pointed out that even in such a case:

1. Arrangements of this sort rarely—the ethical standards of members of Congress being what they are—lead members to vote *against* their convictions; they simply result in the member who is so affected paying a lot of attention to something to which he would otherwise be indifferent.

2. Legally such an arrangement is not a bribe (although, of course, sociologically it is).

Washington representatives in their right minds will ordinarily not themselves engage in any bribing or threatening. To use them for such purposes would be like using a typical university law school teacher to bribe or frighten officials in some backward jurisdiction, so that a young man convicted of a crime would receive either a suspended sentence or special favors while in jail. Prisons being what they are, the young man's friends may resort to such approaches; and there are "fixers" who can help out. But no law school teacher would be likely to "know the ropes" or, even if he did know them, to take the risk.

The parallel is obvious: in both cases, to engage in activity of this sort might destroy a man's professional career. If it became known, such behavior would certainly make future Washington activities extremely difficult because: a. most congressmen and bureaucrats resent efforts to bribe them, and b. in fact (as anybody who is around government for a while learns) most people who threaten do not have the resources to make good on their threats; it simply takes more effort than any interest group can normally muster to implement threats, so a Washington representative who does much threatening is regarded as not believable. And, above everything else, a competent Washington representative does not exaggerate his case much.

Actually, the realization that it is necessary to level with the people one deals with on a day-to-day basis, and the habitual practice of honesty, mean that most Washington representatives would no more bribe or threaten government officials than a professional author would bribe or threaten editors who reject his articles. Honesty and propriety really are the best policies for most Washington representatives.

III.

The seamy side of lobbying and Washington representation has to be discussed because it is so prominent in many people's minds.

But, in fact, quite aside from all false impressions, *there is no reason for most Washington representatives to spend the bulk of their time on legislative lobbying.* As part of the general informational task someone in each Washington office ought to follow committee hearings and the legislative calendar. Clients should be advised when, as, and if relevant legislation will come up, who is introducing it and why, how it will affect them, etc.

Because they have more urgent concerns, many Washington representatives do not pay even this much attention to the Congress. And in some Washington offices the full-time representative is too busy on other government-related problems, so that if necessary the organization hires a lobbying specialist for a particular job. In the larger Washington offices, to be sure, someone does generally follow Congress; but this is not necessarily the most productive task in the office.

Any reader who looks ahead to the list of organizations with Washington interests in the next chapter will grasp one vital point: if a high proportion of organizations with a Washington representative were to engage during each session in intensive lobbying, the whole congressional system would choke up. There simply are not enough congressmen or committees to handle such an input of demands as would then occur. And the number of Washington representatives increases every week.

As the fourth chapter will show, I have no intention of denying the importance of legislative lobbying. But generally the Washington representative acts in a broader framework. A comparison: many people think lawyers spend most of their time in the courtroom, talking to juries; but in reality many attorneys never appear in court, and a majority do their chief work elsewhere. Yet, in stressing this fact, a student of the law is not minimizing the importance of the jury trial.

IV.

DEFINITION OF "WASHINGTON REPRESENTATION."

So far, I have not attempted a definition of Washington representation or of government relations. In suggesting a way of defining Washington representation, for present purposes, it is necessary first to clear away another possible source of confusion. To some firms "our representative in Washington" would mean "our sales manager in Washington." This book is not concerned with the process by which specific sales are made to the government.

Many business firms do have sales representatives in Washington. In fact, many state, municipal, and university representatives in Washington are in the business of arranging for clients to get Federal funds in exchange for specific services or actions. The Port of Seattle, for example, has an agent in Washington so that appropriate Federal authorities may be persuaded to specify that some shipments be made through Seattle. And, as I look back at it, it seems to me that those of us who in 1957 were

planning an upgraded system of Washington representation for
the Commonwealth of Massachusetts were thinking chiefly of
obtaining Federal money for specific services. For instance, I myself had in mind the possibility that the Commonwealth could
get contracts worth several million dollars with the Federal Civil
Defense Administration for research and demonstration projects.
Nowadays any state government is trying to get Federal funds for
highways, health and welfare, education, and so on. Hence any
Washington representative of a state spends much of his time
on grants, contracts, and the direct sale of services.

Faculty members at research-oriented universities, like state
officials, usually have an eye out for Federal support. Ambitious
universities may well use a man in Washington whose main job
is to help get such support—by getting notice of what is desired
and of the preferences of the responsible officials, and of ways to
speed the application process. It is said that some of the newly
established "educational consultants" in Washington even go
so far as to rewrite grant and fellowship applications. I have not
verified this, but it sounds entirely plausible.[5]

Similarly, some veterans' organizations have spent uncounted

[5] In the long run, Federal agencies may find it desirable to limit such
application-writing by others. But at present some Federal requirements are
so complex, and agencies demand such comprehensive methodological statements or reviews of the literature, that applicants will refuse to do the
applications themselves. No doubt the existence of reviewing committees,
each member of which has a different criterion of importance, tends to force
applicants to be more and more comprehensive in their coverage. I myself
have refused to follow up several promising leads to Federal grants, simply
because I did not want to be bothered to develop extensive methodological
statements. Many applicants probably have bothersome things of this sort
handled by junior departmental colleagues, etc., but people at some small
colleges or free lances do not necessarily have such assistance readily available. Hence the tendency to hire specialists to do it. And, of course, a professional, if he or she is really good, will know more about the reviewing
committees and their biases than most scholars, and after a while people at
bigger universities will hire such outside specialists to add the necessary glosses
in the approved style. But this will mean the kind of escalation that takes
place in armaments races, and time spent on preparing applications will become even longer.

hours on case services—helping specific individuals establish or maintain claims to, for instance, disability benefits.

Roughly, I would try to distinguish these *specific* services—sales, case service, grant-getting, contract-making—*where the policy is taken as fixed* from efforts which are concerned with policy formation or modification. Such a distinction is necessarily rough. Anybody engaged in such specific actions may try to get his own organization to change its policy, or he may handle his relations with the government in such a way that the latter changes its policy. Nevertheless, on the one hand, grants, cases, sales may be dealt with as ends in themselves. If this is the approach of a particular person or organization, then he is not engaged in serious Washington representation in the sense in which the word is used in this book.

On the other hand, *some individuals and organizations may be constantly ready to act in regard to policy implications of specific cases and situations; then they are Washington representatives in our sense.*

Naturally, there is a considerable mixture in particular individuals' approaches to the job, and, also naturally, there are intermediate positions between extreme types. Clearly, a district sales manager who merely tries to sell to the government a hundred thousand units of item z is not engaged in Washington representation in our sense. When he begins to report to the head office that it ought to notice that there are undefined policy implications in the purchasing process, he is getting his feet wet. When he takes steps to try to see that someone *acts* with reference to some relevant policy issue, which has not yet been defined in the regulations, he is tending to become a Washington representative.

To illustrate the difficulty of applying the distinction concretely—and to show its significance—contrast the executive officers of two professional associations. The professions in question are very similar. One executive takes regulations and rules and policies for granted except in a few cases where the general body of the association has ordered him formally to protest them.

On the other hand, the executives of the other professional association spend a good deal of time on policy and politics. They take the initiative in regard to National Science Foundation policies, international programs, congressional activities relevant to their field (and to the other field just mentioned, too—for the problems are almost identical). They suggest to government agencies that such-and-such committee meetings be held (and when they are held, the executive of the other association is invited). Of course, they, too, provide individual members of the association with help and assistance in government relations. In fact, they probably give more help, more effectively, than the other; but they are more likely to regard giving advice about how to get a grant as an occasion to think about stimulating some action on policy. The executive officers of this association *evaluate information in political and policy terms*; the executive officer of the other *processes it*. It happens that the second association has developed a larger Washington staff than the first; but one reason it has done so, I judge, is that by taking the initiative it has shown the membership that worthwhile things can be accomplished.

GOVERNMENT RELATIONS.

I have generally talked about "Washington representation." But, in the era of the airplane, many relations with the Federal government can be and are carried on by people whose offices are elsewhere. Indeed, some organizations are reported to keep offices in New York for people who really specialize in Washington representation because they think the staff will then be less visible, look less like nasty lobbyists! But, nasty or not, they practically commute. Numerous officials of corporations, universities, cities, etc., who are not formally assigned to government relations spend a great deal of time on Washington matters.

All these people are engaged in government relations. The difference between them and the Washington representative is often slight; but sometimes it is of considerable significance. The Washington representative is more apt to adopt the professional traditions and the colleague-oriented sentiments of Washington than the government relations man who regards himself as based elsewhere. (Of course, "government relations" does not have to mean relations with the Federal government. It could mean relations with state governments, city governments, the United Nations, or Canada. But nine times out of ten it applies to relations with Federal officials.)

Is it desirable for a government relations specialist to be based in Washington? In general, I think, unequivocally yes. Possibly, a person who has spent several years working for or with government in Washington might have learned the ropes well enough so that he will do well in government relations, even if based elsewhere. But that is to say he has become a member of the Washington community—his reference groups are Washingtonian. I doubt very much whether there is any substitute for learning the Washington atmosphere; only a real political genius can get along as well in government relations without knowing how to handle cues and clues from a Washington point of view. There may be exceptions to this of which I am not aware; in principle, some state governments, some Canadian provinces, Ottawa, the U.N., or perhaps some big national organizations might provide the same sort of training. I can say that I am sure the three other large organizations in which I have had a good deal of experience—the governments of Massachusetts (1957–1961) and Puerto Rico (1944–1965), and the American Unitarian Association (1935–1940)—certainly would not be substitutes for absorbing Washington itself—although experience in the executive departments on Beacon Hill would be very helpful.

However, a man who is Washington-based will usually find

*himself, to some extent, in difficulties with his home-base col-
leagues, clients, or employers.* A representative of a business firm
who acquires Washington viewpoints, or who even tries to explain to top management what Washington's viewpoint is, is
under suspicion. He is no longer one of the group; he is speaking
for an "alien influence," talking "politically" rather than with
business sense. The same thing often happens to representatives
of "cause" groups when they have been in Washington for a
while; whether the cause be better nutrition or conservation or
mental retardation, the grass-roots enthusiastic supporters are
apt to feel that the representative no longer participates whole-
heartedly.

It is not accidental that a Washington representative of a
prominent business firm—who, when he first came on the job,
had the reputation among his colleagues of being very conservative—told me that he is spending more of his time each
month on general social issues; he is apparently favorable to the
objectives of the antipoverty program and feels he should possibly propose some action to his company headquarters. Had he
gone to almost any other slot in the company, he probably would
not have developed in this direction.

Of course, any general rule may have to be modified in particular circumstances. In some cases the chief executive should
handle government relations, but he cannot move to Washington. In other cases, where government relations is not worth the
full time of a qualified man, the person who handles it still should
be a full-time employee of the organization.

There is a good argument for having a rotating system of
Washington representation, if an organization has several people
on its Washington staff—every third or fourth year each man
goes back to headquarters. Numerous other possible exceptions
occur to me, but the point to emphasize is this: The decision
to keep the government relations man at headquarters rather
than in Washington ought to be based on some clear, obvious

advantage.[6] It should never be translatable into the unwillingness of headquarters to relinquish control or be justified in terms of some minor administrative convenience. Effective government relations are worth some inconvenience; if the man who handles them cannot be trusted to operate on his own, he is hardly worth employing in the job.

Finally, *what about the advantages and disadvantages of separating such activities as getting business, applying for grants, and handling cases from real government relations and Washington representation?* First, in the case of business firms one rule is pretty nearly absolute: A sales office which is as much concerned with sales to ordinary purchasers as with those to the government can hardly ever handle government relations in a satisfactory way. Secondly—and conversely—a firm which has a special government sales office can conceivably combine it with the office handling government relations, if nearly all policy problems are with the agencies to which it sells, and if its selling can be quite low pressure. But if many of the firm's problems involve lobbying, for instance, or regulations made by another agency, the mixture probably will not work very well. A sales executive is not a lobbyist, typically, nor is he typically a person who works best and most happily with the specifics of regulations.

It may be that an organization's *main* reason for concern with government relations is *direct* impact upon sales or cases or grants. If one of these is highly crucial and directly justifies the Washington office, presumably the Washington sales or grants office should work closely with the representation office. However, many organizations set up a Washington office which is only incidentally interested in *specific* sales or grants or cases.

---

[6] Interesting along this line is the discussion of headquarters locations in W. L. Warner, D. B. Unwalla, and J. H. Trimm, *The Emergent American Society: Large Organizations*, Vol. I (New Haven: Yale University Press, 1967), especially the material on trade associations in Chapter Nine.

The paper-lumber industry no doubt sells to government; but such matters as air pollution, taxes, quality standards, government research, even anti-discrimination laws are crucial in their Washington relations. Specific sales are secondary. In such cases, the Washington sales office, if there is one, should be quite sharply separated from the representation office; the representatives should be—as in fact they are in that industry—oriented much more to the trade association than to competitive sales. Similarly, although pharmaceutical firms sell millions of dollars worth of goods to the government, general matters like Medicare or the pricing of drugs are far more vital to these firms than are specific sales in Washington.

Universities should generally follow the same sort of procedure. Their Washington representatives certainly can advise faculty members who want research grants what Washington agencies will be interested in particular projects. At times they may suggest ways of restating research problems so that they will appeal more to specific grant-making agencies. But a university Washington representative who spends most of his time working with particular grants—who becomes really a salesman for clients—makes it difficult for the university to get things done in areas more important to it. A specific university will nearly always turn out to be more basically affected by general policy concerning (a) student aid, (b) international education, and (c) university building construction, and by the general policy concerning (d) *kinds* of research grants to be made.

State and municipal representatives seem, so far as I can judge, to have combined the two roles somewhat more successfully. Perhaps this is because they are concerned with matters which are, to some extent, policy matters, even though these also involve grants or contracts. For instance, the decision whether to build the state highway system in a particular way is in fact a policy decision. However, even here my impression is that state and municipal representatives should simply transmit retail or routine matters, and should only get involved themselves, through personal visits or even frequent phone calls, at the wholesale or policy level.[7]

As a Washington staff gets larger, of course, specialization may take care of this sort of problem. Mr. X may spend all his time soliciting research grants for university staff members and canvassing the government (and probably also foundations with offices in Washington); while Mr. Y acts as a genuine Washington representative. But it probably is well to make the lines between them clear, if for no other reason than that Mr. Y should usually and typically work closely with other university representatives on common policy problems, whereas Mr. X, who is to some extent in competition with people from other universities, should be guarded about talking too freely to them about information he picks up!

---

[7] He should, in most cases that is, let the special pleading be done by or at any rate be followed through by the affected department or agency— e.g., he may introduce the people from some small town to the relevant bureau in the government and stand ready to backstop them, if need be. But he will not be the major protagonist for the town's request for aid on some water pollution matter, for instance, particularly if he may have to deal with the same bureau on some general policy matter of regulations affecting grants to control pollution.

2

WHO IS IN GOVERNMENT RELATIONS AND WHY?

I.

One answer to the question "Who is in government relations?" might be "Almost everybody." Just as accounting has become a normal function of any organization of size and complexity, so, nowadays, government relations is coming to be. But different institutions and interests are in government relations in different ways; and some are more likely than others to have representatives in Washington.

It may be useful to list some kinds of interests and associations which are found in Washington—and to comment upon why they are there and how they do their job. These comments will provide a general overview and help to make concrete some of the issues with which this book is concerned. Even those who are themselves engaged in Washington representation may be interested in this view of their profession's ramifications.

The comments also raise several general issues, two of which it may be well to mention now:

1. Why ought some interests to be more active in Washington than they are, in terms of their own purposes?

2. Why are some organizations less heavily represented in Washington than probably would be generally expected?

Consideration of these matters is of general relevance. It could be valuable to:

a. Persons in other organizations or with other interests who wonder about the desirability of setting up a Washington office, and

b. Washington representatives or would-be representatives who are looking for clients. There is more than a joking or selfish interest here; my impression is that the sheer accident of an available, energetic Washington representative who solicits or attracts clients can be quite important politically. If such a representative happens to have solicited or acquired a particular client or clients, potential influence will be actualized.

Obviously, a strong interest—that of the building trades in maintaining prevailing wages on all government-stimulated contracts, or that of the air transport industry in encouraging what is called "a favorable regulatory climate"—will be represented, come hell or high water. But in many cases it is accidental whether a particular interest group, with many problems, many priorities, many possibilities, chooses to be represented in Washington effectively. I would almost guarantee that, now, an aggressive campaign by some impressive person to represent the interests of the nation's suburban areas in Washington would at least speed up—and perhaps make a permanent difference in—special treatment of and concern for suburbs.[1]

Quite likely a similar effort could get greater attention in government programs for tennis players. It is possible, too, that in the mid-1950's the U.S. organ-manufacturing industry would have received more help than it did had it been represented and organized. Certainly it was overlooked as compared with the toy marbles industry and the chicory-growers. It is even imaginable—though not very likely—that gourmets could secure some relevant favors from the government—tax breaks, for example, or the underwriting of research into flavorfulness, or educational grants for master cooks at the same level as grants for graduate study in the sciences.

In sum, "the squeaking wheel gets the grease." Up to a point, and with qualifications, *provided that the squeaking is effectively directed and channelled, rather than random,* this is true in government relations in Washington. The trick is, of course, to have some idea of what kind of squeaking is effective. And that

---

[1] This is no occasion for a treatise on suburbs, as such, but their diversity may serve to illustrate the complexity of Washington representation. For different kinds of suburbs have different kinds of interests in Federal grants and plans. For instance, one type of suburb—the very prosperous outer residential suburb—may chiefly say, in crude summary, "Highway, stay away from our doors! Don't let mass transportation come here." These communities want to keep their exclusive and private character, but other suburbs with large middle- or lower-class populations may be very eager to get support for mass transportation. Therefore, the would-be representative has to pick his potential clients on a specific target basis rather than by the scattershot method. *Actually, targeting is essential to all Washington representation.* In consequence of the need for targeting:

a. few Washington representatives just go out and organize unrepresented clients; unless, by accident, they know Washington and know a particular group of clients, they will not know what the clients specifically need and can get.

b. some "peak associations," such as the U.S. Chamber of Commerce, are proverbially (within the Washington community) regarded as ineffective in lobbying and representation; they cannot effectively target; they have too many diverse constituencies.

is part of the difference between a Washington representative who is competent and one who is not.

II.

Before we consider kinds of interests and organizations which are represented in Washington, a little more on "exceptions" may be worthwhile. By "exceptions" I mean interests or organizations not represented in Washington as actively as seems natural off the bat. The insurance industry, for instance, does not usually concentrate on Washington matters. The reason is that insurance is one of the businesses which are still regulated chiefly by the states;[2] and it comes to Washington most forcefully when there is a possibility of Federal regulation. I have been a little surprised not to find any *very noticeable* traces of separate associations of games players; there are so many golfers, tennis players, etc., that it seems they might be more active in Washington than they are. For instance, urban renewal or model cities programs might be modified to take account of the "national need" for more tennis courts; perhaps we could better match Australia in the Davis Cup competition if we had the same ratio of tennis courts to population. University dormitory facilities grants should provide for attached tennis courts open to the neighboring public. Researchers in health and education ought to pay far more attention than they do (so far as I know) to projects for making tennis even more exciting and even better exercise, so that more people would play it. I suppose players of other games might have similar needs which the Federal government could hope to meet.

---

[2] And where such firms as John Hancock in Boston, for instance, have provided a notable example of how to carry on effective government relations, providing a model which many could profitably imitate.

III.

Washington representation is engaged in by such organizations and interests as these:

LABOR UNIONS.

The most effective "lobby" in the narrow sense in Washington is often said to be the AFL-CIO unions; and many business and other representatives speak of it with envy. In the broader sense —administrative follow-through, public relations, etc.—I don't know that the unions taken as a whole rate quite as high.

"PEAK ASSOCIATIONS" OF VARIOUS SORTS.

The AFL-CIO itself is a peak association, a confederation of unions; the U.S. Chamber of Commerce and the National Association of Manufacturers are also peak confederate groups. It is interesting to note how, in almost every conversation I have ever had in which these are referred to, someone will point out how ineffective the last two are. This is said of the nationals; often it is added that state and/or city chambers or associated industry groups are much more effective allies. The National Association of Trade Association Executives is, as its very name suggests, a peak association. So also are the National Council of Churches and the coalition of patriotic societies (which includes such groups as the Daughters of the American Revolution, the Society of Mayflower Descendants, and the like).

CHURCH GROUPS.

The National Council of Churches and several representatives from moderate, social-action-oriented related church groups seem to have established such a close working relationship that they may be regarded, for practical purposes, as a unit; I think their efforts are mainly lobbying. The Unitarians, on the whole, stand with them, although they adopt a more uncompromising position on Vietnam and race relations. The Catholic groups are regarded by some Federal officials who work with them as having the most astute and skillful representatives. (It does not seem, however, that the ferment of social-action concern among more innovative Catholics, since John XXIII, is adequately represented in Washington yet.) Jewish interests and Jewish concerns are a complex story which it would take years to study; they, I judge, are less predominantly Washington-based than most effective government relations people. Americans United for the Separation of Church and State, a fundamentalist group, may have some weight. And, of course, there are a number of churches —Salvation Army, Mormons, Seventh-Day Adventists—which are different from all the above. The Salvation Army, notably, has a variety of government involvements, for instance, in regard to civil defense.

TRADE ASSOCIATIONS.

Taken altogether, trade associations may represent the widest variety and scope of concerns. Many of them, anyone would guess, must be represented in Washington; but some of the smaller ones—for instance, the National Parking Association (an organization of owners of private parking lots) might not immediately occur to everyone as an organization having a stake in Federal government policy. Yet it is there, actively opposed to the subsidizing or providing of public parking lots as part of an urban renewal program, and, for similar reasons, alarmed about "diversion" of Federal highway funds to build and subsidize parking lots. It could be affected by minimum wage and hour requirements. And, too, its members could, if the matter were handled astutely, profit from programs for creating jobs for un-skilled persons below the poverty line.

Naturally, such industries as pharmaceuticals, paper manu-facturing, coal mining, railroading, and air transport have a wide range of governmental involvements. As an extreme, the air transport industry is a creature of Washington. Everything—policy about rates, policy about airmail subsidies, policy about noise, policy about airport construction, policy about safety, policy about stewardess retirement (note the claim by steward-esses that they are being discriminated against because of age if they are forced to retire in their early thirties), policy about in-ternational flights, policy about special treatment for preferred or prestigous passengers, policy about charter flights—depends upon the government. Since on many of these matters interests are more collective than competitive (although they do com-pete on such matters as route allocation) airlines can do much of what is necessary on a common basis.

The pharmaceutical industry provides, if my interpretation of history is correct, another kind of situation. A dozen years ago this industry was for the most part free of regulation. But a series of developments—including the Kefauver, Humphrey, and Fountain investigations by congressional committees[3]—are mov-ing it toward regulation just as the railroads were pushed under regulation in the latter part of the nineteenth century. But no-body in the industry—and for that matter, few in the govern-ment—stresses or even admits that this is happening. So the Pharmaceutical Manufacturers Association and the representa-tives of the various individual firms are likely to experience troubling days. But for this very reason, the Pharmaceutical Manufacturers Association will become more active (and more firms will have more representatives in Washington), and phar-

[3] See Morton Mintz, *By Prescription Only* (Boston: Little, Brown, 1967), for a report on these hearings and their effects (first edition, 1965, called *The Therapeutic Nightmare*).

maceuticals are likely to be a booming area of government relations.

Such industries as paper manufacturing, textiles, and book publishing will experience fewer extreme stresses in the years immediately ahead, so far as one can see, than pharmaceuticals. But all of them have adequate reasons for needing Washington representation—copyrights, import quotas, labor relations, market or technical research, foreign aid programs, tax matters.[4]

FARM ORGANIZATIONS

The difficulty of any system of classification of Washington representatives is very clearly shown by the farm organizations. Are they a trade association? Are they a professional association? Or a labor union? Some of them have some characteristics of each. Are they even a youth group? Some farm organizations (the 4H Clubs, the Young Farmers of America) purport to represent farm youth, and perhaps do (incidentally like the National Student Association, one of the few such groups which speak for youth in Washington). Are farm organizations part of government? Some are so closely tied in with government that they are hard to separate from it; they have sometimes worked from government offices. But, if they are part of government, they exemplify a point often made—the biggest "lobby" in government, cumulatively, is other government agencies.

---

[4] Political scientists, by the way, have an interesting opportunity for comparative studies of different trade associations. Sometimes a given association has located in Washington for historical or accidental reasons. For instance, it is said that the headquarters of the National Parking Association was initially in Washington simply because the man who founded it lived in Norfolk, Virginia, and the association of mobile food caterers is, I judge, in Washington also because of the accident of location of the founder. Has location materially altered the orientation of the Parking Association? Will it alter that of the mobile food caterers?

Anyway, the farm associations are there—and they are rather influential in agricultural policy. The outsider may not realize how much, formally and informally, these groups divide along commodity lines—dairy, tobacco, cotton, etc.

BUSINESS FIRMS.

Of course, many individual business firms have Washington representation. Where there is a Washington-based trade association, the association and Washington representatives of the industries in the association typically work together in alliance. But any particular firm is likely to have its own special interests or points of view. Many textile manufacturers will probably support an import quota in 1968; but some textile manufacturers, either directly through the firm, or indirectly through the owners, have foreign interests which lead in a different direction. And since there are many differences among the markets for different textile products, some textile manufacturers may not be at all hurt by imports, while others will suffer. (In 1953–1955, when I was concerned with the textile business, it seemed that U.S. producers of cheap goods, and U.S. producers of expensive ones, were or could be hurt by foreign competition, while middle-range producers were not as subject to underselling by attractive foreign goods.)

And something may be extremely important to a particular firm which matters far less to its competitors. Many paper manufacturers may be affected to some extent by air pollution control regulations; but the precise location of their plants and the exact chemistry of their processes will make a good deal of difference to how important the regulations are to any given firm.

Then, too, particular firms may, for historical or institutional reasons, be much affected by something which is of no concern to competitors. Congressman Wright Patman, through the committee of which he is chairman, has been looking for some years into foundation and business ownership. Many pharmaceutical firms have no particular reason to follow his investigations, as far as I know; but Eli Lilly (much of the stock of which is in foundation hands) and its Washington representative might be affected. There have been times, too, when Ford might have been vitally interested in these investigations, but they probably matter less to the other three automobile-makers. But General Motors (and also Maremont) must necessarily want to follow antitrust activities within the Department of Justice very closely, whereas these may not, at the moment, be so significant to American Motors. Or a particular textile manufacturer might envision some way in which he could get in on the automobile seat belt business or on other safety features of automobile supplying—so he will follow the actions of regulatory agencies and perhaps try to influence them, while his competitors in general textiles will barely have heard of the situation.

ETHNIC MINORITY PROTEST OR DEFENSE GROUPS.

Negro, Jewish (overlapping the religious category), Japanese-American, Mexican-American, American Indian, etc.

FOREIGN GOVERNMENTS.

A number of foreign governments maintain Washington offices that are more or less independent of their ambassadors—for instance, a trade council in Washington has close ties with the ministry concerned with foreign trade, while its relations to the foreign office are less close.

In other cases, a commercial attaché, or, indeed, the ambassador himself, may be engaged in trying to communicate to or get information about U.S. trade, aid, health, education, and welfare grants, fiscal policy, and a variety of other matters, or to exert influence on these matters. In effect, in these cases the embassy is doing just about the same sorts of things which the representative of a state government does. The most obvious difference is that embassies are less likely to lobby before Congress. Lobbying, or any potentially offensive attempt to influence public opinion, is apt to be conducted for them by Americans. The trade council just mentioned is staffed entirely by Americans.

This is not to say that the only, or even the main, job of an embassy staff is to engage in Washington representation in the sense in which it is discussed in this book. Diplomacy in the chaotic international world takes account of many issues and of relationships not typically found within the United States. But after all, there was a time when the American sugar price—set by the United States government, rather than by the market— mattered more to Cuba than all other diplomatic and economic factors put together. And Taiwan and Pakistan and Turkey all have been heavily dependent upon American aid—so that if they can present their cases to sympathetic ears at the Pentagon or at Commerce or on Capitol Hill, why should they not?

I do not myself know of representation in Washington— except by would-be separatist or breakaway groups—of foreign provinces or opposition parties. It may be that I have simply overlooked this; I am sure, however, that if I were seeking clients for a Washington representative office, I would approach Premier Smallwood of Newfoundland, Premier Robichaud of New Brunswick, and the premiers of Nova Scotia and Prince Edward Island. Eastern Canada is as intimately affected by many Washington decisions—for example, those affecting the fishing industry and fishing research—as is the United States. New Brunswick, Nova Scotia, and Newfoundland have sent thousands of their people to what they used to call "the Boston States"—and from the standpoint of educational research and mental health research, the Washington government has just as much reason to be interested in them as in Puerto Rico. (Puerto Rico does, of course, have active Washington representation.)

Indeed, in almost any industrialized nation, there are local or special interests which are affected by Washington, and to which some agency in Washington might respond on a special basis. At some time, for example, the balance of payments situation may lead the United States really to restrict tourist travel in most of Europe; it is conceivable that people in Scotland, foreseeing this prospect, would do well to set up a Washington office of their own now—to take advantage of the special sentimental feeling many persons of Scottish descent have about the old country, and to make clear that Scotland is a much, much more impoverished area than southern Great Britain, so that special arrangements could be made to permit tourists in the habit of going to northern Britain to continue, despite general restrictions on tourism.

STATE GOVERNMENTS, ASSOCIATIONS OF STATE AND/OR
CITY OFFICERS, ASSOCIATIONS OF MUNICIPALITIES, AND
CITY GOVERNMENTS.

One possible consequence of Great Society legislation may be an increase in the power of the governor in each state, so that the governorship indeed controls other agencies. It would very much simplify the Federal-state relations situation if this came to pass. (I myself have enough faith in the individualism of American politics to think that Great Society pressures in this direction will not, on the whole, succeed.) In most states, anyhow, there are now agencies that are practically, and sometimes theoretically, independent of the governor. In Florida, the governor is from some standpoints simply one member of an elected "cabinet," but with this important difference: other members can be, and usually are, reelected—many serve four or five terms—while the governor is forbidden reelection. In Massachusetts, when the Furcolo administration came into office in 1957, we could not even find an accurate list or count of the agencies that were in practice independent and reported only to the governor. The

number was in the hundreds. (This situation has been clarified
since that date.)

In principle, any one of the independent, autonomous agencies in some states could—if it had the funds—have its own
Washington representative. Of course, some agencies have so
little to do with Washington directly, or their business is so
routine, that this would not make a great deal of sense;[5] however, it has long been surprising to me, considering the necessity
some state politicians are under to create sinecures, that there
are not more such positions than in fact exist. But many agencies
do have a good deal to do with Washington; and one of the two
gravest obstacles to the Furcolo administration's proposal to
appoint a Washington representative directly responsible to the
governor came from state agencies which already had their own
communications with Washington. They were, naturally, fearful
that we would cut their existing pipelines. (Since then, Governor
Volpe appointed a representative who is really responsible to him
—although subsequently legislative approval of the continua-
tion of this post was denied.) Associations of state agencies do
operate extensively in Washington—and necessarily, at various
times, they operate against the programs and emphases of particular governors. The American Public Welfare Association, for
instance, is recognized as extremely effective within its scope.
Its membership also includes local welfare officials. The North
American Association of Alcoholism Commissioners has recently
been engaged in pushing for an upgrading of the Federal alco-

---

[5] However, in a series of interviews with officials of about 60 state government agencies in Massachusetts in 1957–1959 (as part of a project directed by the late Morton Grodzins), it became apparent that almost every
agency was dependent upon Washington (or occasionally upon some national association which had taken the place of Washington) and that the
biggest variable in the matter was how much I knew about the particular
agency. *The more I knew about the agency, the more it turned out its
official remembered about its relationships with Washington—because then
I knew enough to ask pertinent questions.*

holism studies center and in cooperating in the drafting of alcoholism legislation. This association does begin to approach my
suggestion that Canadian provinces might be represented in
Washington, for its membership includes, as the title implies,
alcoholism commissioners from Canadian provinces as well as
from the United States. Some people outside the group say that
alcoholism officials from Ontario probably have more weight in
the association than do those from any single state. It is even
more than *inter*national; although it represents state and pro-
vincial agencies which contribute to its support, about half of its
funds, I was told, actually come from a private foundation.

Then, too, there is the association of state mental health
program officers, the National Association of State Civil Defense
Directors, the National Guard organization, the association of
state highway officials, etc., etc.—which merge and overlap with
professional associations on the one hand and municipal or
county groups on the other.

There are several associations of municipal officials, representing rather different interests and emphases in the urban
picture; the mayors' conference, for example, is said to stress the
problems of a different kind of municipality than does the
municipal association. Some of the large cities have Washington representatives as such; others are frequently represented in
Washington by the mayor or somebody on his staff. My impression is that, on the whole, suburban areas do not yet have
Washington representation in proportion to their needs and potential demands. Probably this is due to a lag in forming *associations* of suburban officials. Evidently, it would not be worthwhile
on an individual basis for each suburb of Boston and New York
and Chicago to have its own representative in Washington. It
is also possible that even now a good many suburbs are represented by different attorneys or Washington specialists on a retainer basis—and that I simply have not heard about them.

PROFESSIONAL ASSOCIATIONS.

State and municipal representation overlaps that of professional associations. A large number of members of the American Association on Mental Deficiency, which is a professional association, are employed by states or school districts. Consequently, therefore, this association often does the same kinds of things in its area, as, say the Association of Land Grant Colleges does in its area. But the latter is not exactly a professional association. To anyone who knows the geography of Washington, it is significant, in terms of the point that "it isn't just lobbying," that the Association on Mental Deficiency (which established a Washington office only recently) has its headquarters out at 5201 Connecticut Avenue. This location is more accessible to the National Institutes of Health than to the Congress.

More often than not, the National Association of Social Workers is apt to share interests with the American Public Welfare Association. The APW would, of course, be less likely than the NASW to get into general social action (civil rights or contraception some years ago, now the Vietnam War); naturally, too, the APW would be less apt than the NASW to speak for rank-and-file movements in the social work profession on some matter which involved opposition to state headquarters!

Then there is the American Medical Association, which represents the self-employed practitioner rather more than the physician employed by a state agency. On the one hand, AMA is concerned with a very substantial number of measures in Congress; on the other, there are hundreds of programs being carried on by Federal agencies that are of interest to doctors—or for which their professional advice is desired and solicited, so that an approach may be legitimized or future bother avoided. Naturally, there are associations for nurses and home economists (both the

Departments of Agriculture and Health, Education, and Welfare are active in fields important to home economists), and so on and so forth.

Political scientists who read this book probably know that an active professional association in Washington is the American Political Science Association. In fact, what is in a way a companion volume to this book, *The Job of the Congressman*, by Donald Tacheron and Morris Udall (Bobbs-Merrill, 1966), was an outgrowth of a characteristic American Political Science Association project. Along similar lines, the Association runs internship programs for younger political scientists, journalists, civil servants, and also for a few state legislators, Asiatic and European parliamentarians, and so forth. Of course, the management and financing of these projects involves constant relationships with government.

Other social science professions also have Washington headquarters. One of their executive secretaries stated that he spends much time supplying to government the names of people who can serve on committees, undertake various assignments, etc. This is, of course, the business of *giving to government information* which it is also useful for the interest group to let government have. I judge that in this case probably at least 95 percent of requests for this kind of information come from the bureaucracy rather than from the Congress.

EDUCATION.

Naturally, there has been a considerable growth in the contacts between representatives of educational groups and the Federal government in recent years. Any reader of this book is likely to be aware of the increased Federal involvement in education. Universities send representatives of their own to Washington, professional associations spend more time there, firms of educational consultants spring up. (What is a school board to do when it needs guidance through the maze of Washington bureaucracy, where everybody refers familiarly to statutes and regulations by number?) Just at present, one hears complaints from some of the more experienced Washington representatives in this field; they say it is harder to get to see top people. Not surprisingly, for top people have far more responsibilities and programs to administer than used to be the case. And, vice versa, one hears interesting complaints from the Department of Health, Education, and Welfare; down there they say that while the Department has recently brought in new, innovative, pioneering people—"quite unlike those who ran the old Office of Education"—the organizations are still making do with the kind of representatives who used to negotiate with the old office, and that these people do not speak the language of innovation and pioneering and so forth. Whether either of these interpretations has merit, I cannot pretend to judge; but there may be a failure of fit somewhere. (This may change under Finch.)

RESEARCH.

Education suggests research. Researchers are in fact represented in Washington through professional associations, etc.

But research can also be a *form* for interest-group expression. The Brookings Institution certainly has a good deal of influence in government, and to some extent it probably does represent an "intellectual establishment." More obviously oriented toward a specific policy line is the American Enterprise Institute of Public Policy, which tends to produce first-rate research offsetting the prevailing "liberal ideology" of the social science research "establishment." It is natural that its orientation is more obvious; simply because the prevailing emphasis of the "establishment" is "liberal," a conservative (or a Marxist) group is more likely to stand out and develop its own research agency than is a "liberal" group.

It is sometimes hard to distinguish a cause from a hobby, for one man's hobby is another man's cause. There are, for example, several different associations and organizations concerned with conservation, the preservation of wild life, unspoiled natural space, etc. To some, this is a crusade; to others, a hobby. In any event, these groups campaign for setting aside national park-land, preventing the destruction of wetlands, preserving egrets, eagles, redwood trees, and the like. Sometimes this involves lobbying, but a great many of the meetings, hearings, petitions, and pleas are directed to one administrative agency or another. It is certainly, for instance, far more direct to try to persuade the Air Force not to destroy a bird sanctuary, or to encourage engineers or agronomists from Defense or Agriculture to leave some natural space unspoiled, than to try to persuade Congress to prohibit such actions.

Similarly with issues of patriotism; there is a coalition of patriotic societies, some of whose members regard themselves as engaged in a veritable crusade. They resemble but are very different from associations eager to prevent the destruction of historic landmarks, most of whose members probably participate as a hobby.

In the social welfare field, of course, there are many interest groups which support a cause. Historically, the temperance societies have stood out as remarkably aggressive and effective; their vigor is somewhat abated nowadays. Of a somewhat similar type —although with only a fraction of the strength—is the National Health Foundation, a major activity of which is trying to make sure that attention is given to its argument against destroying the nutritional value of foods by use of artificial preservatives and protections. And there are those concerned with kindness to animals. (In one session of Congress, more letters were probably received about the slaughter of wild horses than about any other issue except postal pay raises!)

Arising from the same general motivation are the groups to protect the handicapped and diseased—which spill over into professional associations. The American Association on Mental Deficiency has long represented the professionals in the field; the National Association for Retarded Children, on the other hand, has usually been more aggressive and demanding, less ready to accept any priority attached to competing interests. It has been more passionate because it was founded by parents of retarded children. Its style has moderated as its staff became professional and as retardation became a fashionable cause, so that some of its members and leaders were not of necessity personally involved. Some similar sort of representation is given by other groups interested in the handicapped; probably best known is the "March of Dimes," which originally attacked infantile paralysis. Is the National Association of Retired Persons a "cause" or a status group?

The "cause" groups currently receiving the most attention, of course, are those opposed to the Vietnam War. For reasons pointed out later, they can gain or think they can gain little from approaches to the executive branch; so, for the most part, they must either lobby or resort to public demonstration.

General civic groups. The League of Women Voters is the outstanding example.[6]

Student groups.

Fraternal organizations.

Veterans organizations.

Government employees.

Two groups may or may not belong in this classification logically; although many members of Congress and some govern-

---

[6] See R. Bauer, I. Pool, and L. Dexter, *American Business and Public Policy*, chapter 27, "The Ladies of the League."

ment agencies hear more from them than from any other groups. Veterans, in a sense, are exgovernment employees concerned with personnel policy (pensions, etc.); government employees are concerned chiefly with personnel problems. It seems to me that government employees do not fit logically into the same category as these other groups. Their relationship to the Bureau of the Budget or to the Congress or to the Civil Service Commission or to the postmaster general is not typically political in the same sense. To be sure, they are concerned with policy, but only policy in the sense that any employee who wants a pay raise or better working conditions is concerned with policy. There is some sentiment and concern in one or two Federal employee groups which goes beyond the conditions of labor, but it is not major. If we had unions of Federal employees aggressively concerned with changing policy matters as such—if, for instance, the postal workers became disgusted with the urban sprawl they see every day and wanted the government to do something about that, or if a union of forest service workers insisted that their superiors take account of certain views they hold about resources management—then the Federal employee groups would be engaged in government relations in our sense. (The nearest thing to this, to my knowledge, is to be found in the situation immediately after World War II, when scientists who had been working on what were directly governmental projects took a strong stand on the control of atomic energy.) As it is, most government employee groups are chiefly involved in personnel matters.

Some people also emphasize what is, of course, quite true, that there is a great amount of influence by government agencies upon one another. This is shown in one respect by the appointment in most agencies of legislative liaison specialists (agency lobbyists). But, beyond that, Treasury tries to "lobby" State, Agriculture to influence Interior, and so on.

In conclusion, it is probably important to stress what is referred to several times in this chapter. There are—certainly—a number of occasions in which people are engaged in trying to get the government to do something by means that are more or less corrupt, unethical, illegal. Any reader of the *New York Times* or *Life Magazine* will be familiar with a number of allegations and accounts of such efforts. In general, efforts of this type tend to be focused upon getting specific considerations, specific deviations from established policy, special favors, rather than focusing upon trying to change policy. To the extent that this is the case, these efforts would not in themselves fall within the definition of government relations which I have suggested is useful. Unquestionably, there is no moral or organizational code under which people trying to "corrupt" the government refrain from attempting to alter policy; but, in fact, in the nature of the case, efforts to alter policy are, within the American system of government, mostly conducted above the table—since it is widely recognized and believed that any one is free to try to alter established policies. So that for the most part, issues of graft and corruption do not, directly at least, bear upon the practice of government relations as here defined and described.

Naturally, the issue is not as simple as the preceding paragraph suggests; in the first place those agencies and people concerned with relationship with those agencies where "graft and corruption" are to be expected, are influenced by the total organizational climate. To name an agency which is not now in the news, the Alien Property Custodian; all dealing with it in the late 1940's must have been influenced by the belief, or the fact, that there was a considerable amount of sharp practice and favoritism in connection with its decisions. In the second place, efforts to change policy, conducted by persons who are accustomed to sharp practice and the getting of special favors, often involve bribery, threats, or attempted bribery or threats—because this is the way these people are accustomed to doing business. (One of the things which recurrently surprises people in some aspects of state government in some states is the frequency with which bribes are hinted at where there is no necessity for and considerable disadvantage in making the hint.) In the third place, the expectation that things are being done dishonestly affects attention, to reporting of, and interpretation of policy decisions.

Granted all the points just made, nevertheless, most practitioners of government relations at the Federal level never or very rarely come into contact with anything where bribes or threats of a sort widely considered illegitimate are involved; and most important policy decisions by the Federal government are made without any recourse to bribes, attempted bribery, or threats. It would, probably, be an interesting and worthwhile enterprise to discuss those areas of Federal government where bribes and threats are at present commonly used; but this is not the significant issue at hand; and there may not be any of great significance.

3

MEANS AND CHANNELS
OF GOVERNMENT
RELATIONS

Any well-planned government relations program soon comes up against the problem: For the purposes in view, what are the best access routes, the best channels for influencing government?

In the United States system of government and politics, this can be a very complicated question. As the late Morton Grodzins often pointed out, *the American system of government is pre-eminently a system of "multiple cracks," multiple access points.* For a given purpose and interest, the best access may be through the Congress; that is, the situation may really call for lobbying. But if so, the question then becomes: Does it make any difference

which committees are approached? Most matters *can* be handled
by any one of several committees. Should the approach be
through the legislative or the appropriations or the investigatory
process?[1]

But it may be that the most effective route is through one or
another of the executive departments. The decision as to which
department(s) and bureau(s) to approach may take much reflection and study. Or some problems can best be tackled through
regulatory commissions—the Interstate Commerce Commission,
the Federal Communications Commission, etc. And, naturally,
there are some matters on which the White House itself might
take favorable action.

Too it is often worth seeing whether the courts are a good
means of getting a handle on a problem. Although many Washington representatives and government relations men are attorneys by training, there seems to be little tendency to look at
court action and litigation as an alternate way of influencing
government policy. Yet, anyone who thinks about the historic
effort of Thurgood Marshall and the legal staff of the National
Association for the Advancement of Colored People will see
that lawsuits were a major route toward Negro equality. In some
of these cases, the attorneys for the NAACP helped to make law
—because they raised new questions for judges and/or helped
judges formulate new answers. So, also, the reapportionment
issue had been raised in other ways for years. But a determined
effort did bring the matter into the courts again; and they did
give the desired decisions. Just now, the country may be on the
verge of seeing implementation of some objectives of prison re-
formers as a result of court action. Of course, all these issues are
basic enough so that the Supreme Court was able to handle them
in terms of constitutional doctrine.

[1] On the question how to handle the Congress, see Bertram Gross, *The
Legislative Struggle* (New York: McGraw-Hill, 1953).

But there are numerous instances where associations and interests might get satisfaction through the lower courts—if they planned adequately. Certainly, my general impression in regard to the complaints of business men with whom I talked during two different studies was that they were unaware of legal reliefs for some of their problems with government. For instance, in listening to criticisms of reciprocal trade, I heard some of the most bitter complaints about matters which could have been handled under existing laws. Relief might have been obtained through actions by the Tariff Commission or the Treasury acting in a quasijudicial fashion. If these agencies did not supply relief, it is likely that an ingenious attorney could have discovered ways of bringing some of the issues (if they had real merit) before the courts.[2]

And in interviewing a number of business executives about how (if at all) they and their firms took part in politics, I heard a number of complaints about alleged unfairnesses of government. It seemed to me that some of these complaints were valid; but, if they were serious, there were probably legal ways of dealing with some of them. But at that time (in 1960) business-in-politics was

[2] Unfortunately, at the time I was taking part in these studies, I was not aware of this problem, so I made no special note or record which would prove anything. I rely, therefore, upon a general impression. So far as the tariff and reciprocal trade go, anyone who wants to undertake the (incredibly dull) job of analyzing hearings before Senate Finance (and Labor) and House Ways and Means on reciprocal trade matters could probably test the impression. That would take as much time as writing this book, which is why I have not done it.

Of course, legal action sometimes demands a long, tiresome, bothersome, expensive process. But, similarly, an adequate government relations program is expensive in money and time. There is probably one difference between writing one's congressman, etc., and going to law. One can write a letter or even make a personal complaint to a congressman or bureaucrat without intending to do more than express anger and annoyance. But once a lawsuit is set in motion, it seems to have an independent life of its own.

Following from the above is the observation that some people regard a Washington representative as someone who can tell the government where it should "get off" and do not want a serious, planned program.

the fashion of the year among up-to-date executives. They saw these complaints as showing exclusively, as far as I could tell, the necessity for electing better congressmen, possibly lobbying, etc.,[3] but apparently they did not consult their law departments on these issues.

I.

A government relations program should be planned with a view to taking appropriate steps on Capitol Hill, through the Congress, and/or through the executive departments, and/or through the White House, and/or through the regulatory agencies, and/or through the Federal courts.

Fortunately, this is not usually as complicated as it sounds. In actual practice, many Washington representatives are well guided by experience and do not have to think through the alternatives open to them in each new case. But government relations men who have not had Washington experience—and a good many Washington representatives—may not in fact choose the most promising access route. They tend to approach the government agencies which they know best or about which they have heard the most. Usually this leads to the correct decision; but there can be crucial occasions when it results in a mistake. For instance, government relations specialists who have the idea, whether from their own experience or from the greater publicity given to legislation, that Congress is the place to start may be right most of the time—but if they are wrong, they are not doing as well for their clients as they ought.

---

[3] As I look back, none of the (very responsible and senior) officers of the (really major) corporations with whom I talked so much as mentioned a Washington office or a government relations program. Since I encourage interviewees to talk about anything that seems to them relevant, it is likely that if any substantial proportion of them had much interest in a government relations program, certainly if they regarded it as relevant, they would have mentioned it. It would be valuable to undertake similar interviews in 1969, and see if government relations is mentioned.

Obviously, a client or employer looking for a Washington representative or a director of a government relations program should seek someone who is not wedded to any particular access route or technique. There is a danger in hiring men who have worked for some particular agency. They are inclined to look at that agency as the normal access route and to think its point of view toward other agencies or unfamiliar techniques to be the only normal one. I have seen Washington representatives whose background was in a "very proper" bureau treat with real disdain the idea that some particular matter could best be handled through the Congress, or—heaven forbid!—through a public relations effort. They felt that the proper thing to do was to talk problems over, as expert to expert, at a cocktail hour or lunch and get them settled. They felt those "clowns" on Capitol Hill could be of no use. Conversely, I have seen Washington representatives whose experience had been entirely with the Congress utterly fail to realize that in their situation bringing in any congressman, no matter how prominent, would look like "pressure" to bureaucrats whose good will was necessary.[4]

The difference between a Washington representative who benefits from the training he has received in Washington and

[4] Although not a situation where (as far as I know) any Washington representation was involved, it may help to show the negative side of congressional involvement to report the following: In connection with certain specialized kinds of manpower assignments, advantageous to the assignee, during a war a certain government official had to OK them. On one occasion, I saw him turn two out of 30 properly requested applications for such assignment. Why were these two turned down, I asked? "Didn't you see?" he said. "Senator X wrote us about case Y and Congressman R about Case Z. They were trying to pressure us. That'll show 'em!" As far as anybody could tell from the letters, the Senator and the Congressman really did know personally the man about whom they wrote.

Later, a distinguished magazine editor, who had invited me to write an article for his magazine, refused to meet me in the office of Congressman R. W. Bolling where I then had the use of a desk: "I don't have anything to do with politicians," he said. But it never occurred to him to object to meeting me in another office, the funds for which came from Defense Department research contracts, although the article did deal with Defense Department policies and had no relationship to any especial concern of Congressman Bolling's!

one who suffers from "trained incapacity" lies in this: A *competent government relations man regards his main responsibility as the achievement of what are in the broad sense* political *purposes for his client. He knows that, to the limit of his time and skills, and ethical obligations, he should consider whatever techniques and access routes will be useful to the client; and within the limits of what is practical, he is prepared to tell his client when he lacks the most relevant kind of knowledge or the appropriate technical skills.*

Whether this point of view can be lived up to, of course, depends upon the client. In principle, it is similar to the professional obligation of a lawyer or a doctor. A diagnostician, who has never done surgery, refers the patient to a skilled surgeon; an attorney, who has never been engaged in patent or tax work, tells the client what kind of practitioner to look for.[5] A sophisticated client should welcome a professional man who takes this point of view; but the client should be able to say, in the case of Washington representation, "For reasons of cost" or "Because you are already familiar with the situation, I'll ask you to handle that end of it, and I will realize that you warned me."

II.

There is a real difficulty in trying to regard the full range of government as the task, rather than concentrating upon some particular part of it. There is more of a difficulty in remembering, constantly, that government relations programs ought to take into account, not just the Federal government, but what some political scientists call "the entire polity." By the "polity" is meant

----

[5] Or to give a still more relevant but less familiar example: A person engaged in lobbying on state matters in a given state, confronting a situation which spills over into another state, if he has any sense of effectiveness and ethics at all, will examine the situation carefully to see whether some "native son," whose base is in the politics of the second state, should be hired as a consultant—at least to provide a front.

the entire act of organizations and major influences, whatever they are called, which do in fact direct and govern life in the manner of the national state (the Federal government).

For convenience, we can divide aspects of the polity likely to be important in some government relations program as follows:

I. Non-Governmental

    A. Media, public relations, etc. (*but note we are talking about public relations geared into political and policy objectives*, which is different from much of public relations and publicity), both mass and special.

    B. Big national organizations

    C. Organizations not necessarily big but key to a given situation.

    D. Possible allies or enemies.

II. Other governments

    A. State and local

    B. International (U.N., and others)

    C. Foreign

Whoever does the overall government relations planning and thinking, the basic principles are: (a) *that the organization is trying to bring about or resist some contemplated change* and (b) *although the Federal government is, as a whole, the most powerful institution in the polity,* (c) *it is not exclusively powerful; in certain situations these other organizations can and do play a very significant part* and (d) *sometimes, the strategy of the indirect approach has more influence on the Federal government than an exclusive effort trying to influence it directly.*

MULTIPLE CRACKS IN THE POLITY.

These last two points extend Grodzins' notion of the United States government as a system of "multiple cracks" one step further. They lead to the notion that the entire U.S. *polity* is a system of "multiple cracks," multiple access routes. And, from the standpoint of the Washington representative, this means that he ought to take into account all the promising access routes (granted of course natural limitations due to time and energy) whether in or outside the government—that is to say, as many as he can.

STRATEGY OF THE INDIRECT APPROACH.

A word about the last point (d) above, the strategy of the indirect approach. In some cases, it is obvious enough. For instance, if in 1957 advocates of birth control and planned parenthood could have obtained support from, or even diminished resistance by, the American Catholic hierarchy or from politicians in heavily Catholic states, they would have materially increased the likelihood that the Federal government (HEW, AID, the Department of Defense) would sponsor birth control programs. Consequently, it might well have been that, instead of devoting a lot of effort to direct Washington representation in 1957, advocates of such programs would have been wiser to focus on overcoming resistance in Massachusetts and Rhode Island, or among some clerical leaders. Actually, there would have been other points to consider in this case, but in reverse the situation is clear. Those opposed to birth control programs, for whatever reason, should have tried to strengthen manifestations of opposition to it within the Catholic states of Massachusetts, Rhode Island, and Connecticut.[6]

---

[6] It probably should be added that the *appearance* of popular concern is often, on secondary issues, sufficient to influence Washington. In R. Bauer, I. Pool, and L. Dexter, *American Business and Public Policy* (New York: Atherton, 1963), we report a situation where in "New Anglia" there was a strong impression outside the community that people in the community were deeply concerned about the threat of a quota on residual fuel oil. In fact, local involvement was very slight and largely manufactured from outside. "New Anglia did not know that it was thought of as the heart of the fight on the Simpson Bill. It knew that it was merely giving mild cooperation to a push from outside, but it did not know whence this push came. . . . The

There are less obvious instances of the uses of the indirect approach to the Federal government. If some large manufacturers are persuaded—or coerced by municipal ordinances—into handling their own pollutants which would otherwise go into air and water, it will cost them money. They will feel it unfair and unreasonable that other manufacturers—particularly competitors—are able to keep costs down because these others continue to pollute the atmosphere and the rivers. They will therefore be likely to support programs designed to reduce pollution generally.

A group of Citizens for Clean Water or Clean Air would, presumably, support *Federal* agencies and *Federal* action. But they might effectively devote a good deal of their short-run effort to municipal ordinances in certain industrial cities or to influencing management of some large industries to act against pollution. Two circumstances under which management might be susceptible to such influence are: 1. big companies where the top managers have respiratory disorders causing suffering from dirty air, and 2. big companies where the managers are interested in preserving fish, which are killed by pollutants in streams.

"POWER OF THE PRESS."

Similarly, there is certainly a vast amount of exaggeration as to the "power of the press,"[7] etc., in political discussion. But the press and TV can, sometimes, get or keep attention focused on scandals, lead people to get excited, so that there is a call for some sort of action. The effectiveness or ineffectiveness of newspaper

---

communications (however) fitted the Congressmen's image of reality . . . so when the Congressmen heard what seemed to be the voice of community feeling, they accepted it as such." (pp. 294–295)

[7] See Lewis A. Dexter and David M. White, *People, Society, and Mass Communications* (New York: Free Press, 1964). In general, the press is a powerful focuser of attention and selector of channels for action, although with little influence (once attention and selection has taken place) on outcomes.

stories from the standpoint of ultimate political results, is partly a matter of interpretation, and partly a matter of the ability of the people interested in a cause to provide a sensationally dramatic demonstration. It would seem possible, for instance, to do more than has been done with sensational, dramatic accounts of individuals—preferably children—actually choking to death as a result of dirty air. And such stories, repeated in different places, might do more to help the implementation of Clean Air Acts than a direct lobbying campaign for more funds or more "teeth" in the act. Some congressional investigations are effective, because they lead to publicity, which in turn leads to a demand for action; this seems to have been the case with recent ones about local packers and dirty meat.

SPECIALIZED PRESS.

So far, I have been speaking, evidently, of the popular press. But, in regard to some matters, there is a specialized or professional press which might be influenced. One question to ask—I have no idea as to the answer—in regard to air pollution is whether there are technical journals, read by engineering executives, which are relevant. It could well be, for instance, that appropriate articles in such journals would persuade engineers to reduce their opposition to compulsory legislation and/or make them feel that the company really ought to do something about the matter.[8] It is surely the case that advocates of cleaner air might have done more in the medical, nursing, etc., press than in fact they have. Such an emphasis might have led to somewhat more interest in the matter by medical groups than has in fact been manifest.

---

[8] An impression—derived from a family business, constructed on patents for air pollution devices, and later, from interviews with engineers in several southern cities, on related matters—is that a very big obstacle to the initiation of air pollution programs is, or was, the feeling of engineers: None of our business; adds to production costs; it's the government interfering.

THE STATES.

Going back to the states, in the last few years, people have become accustomed to thinking of the Federal government as the pioneer—with the states sometimes imitating. But in the history of the Republic, Massachusetts, New York, and Wisconsin, for instance, have pioneered a number of developments which were later imitated by the Federal government and other states.

BUSINESS AND THE POLITY.

On the whole, it is hard to think of current matters involving business which could profitably be initiated in the states or the press as a means of affecting Washington. But the reason for this is simply that a large part of business representation is "defensive"—to try to prevent government from interfering or making trouble. In those cases, in which business representatives are concerned with a *positive* program, they need to take into account the rest of the polity, just as much.

KEY ASSOCIATIONS.

By "Key associations" which are not necessarily large or influential in themselves, I would have in mind, for instance, engineering associations in the Clean Air matter.

More generally, if there is no vehement protest against it from some sources, it is frequently important to disarm or nullify potential opponents beforehand. If I am at all correct, for example, the current sentiment in the country is in favor of more effective detective methods and of more stringent measures against suspects. But the outcry from a few groups, the American Civil Liberties Union and the American Unitarian Association, for instance, will be great, if efforts are made to introduce wiretaps more generally, to question suspects more harshly, and so on.

Influencing these groups—if you like, "lobbying" the ACLU and AUA—is almost a "must" for opponents of recent Supreme Court policies. It is interesting that, so far as I know, police associations have not been especially effective in Washington or in state capitals nor has the movement to support your local police been particularly effective on specifics. If these last groups should move from the expression of indignation and disgust to political effectiveness, one thing they ought to try to do would be to disarm the liberal interests, just mentioned. And, in fact, this might well be achieved; there is not as great a chasm between the two sides as appears at first glance.

This is, of course, a case of moderating opposition. But there are other instances where associations are in fact "keys" simply because influential people pay attention to them and need them. The simplest and clearest example of a "key association" is the Massachusetts Taxpayers Association; for years, it has been the best—on some matters, nearly the only—source of information and (relatively liberal) guidance on the administration and structure of that state's government. Consequently, many people in the state, who count, pay attention to it. There are similar, although less completely apparent, cases in the national government.

UNITED NATIONS, CANADA, AND OTHERS.

A classic instance of the way in which a foreign government influenced the United States is to be found in the two Migratory Birds cases. The Supreme Court first declared a law null and void affecting migratory birds. Then the administration negotiated and the Senate ratified a treaty with Canada, containing approximately the same provisions. Since this was now in the field of foreign affairs, the Court found the Treaty constitutional. But supposing there had been some doubt about Canadian action in the matter? Then Ottawa representation would have been the road to Washington effectiveness—for conservationists.

Beyond our relationships with Canada, there are a good many matters where effective accomplishment depends upon influencing a foreign government. It was said at the time—although it was one of the issues which we neglected in the Bauer-Pool-Dexter study of reciprocal trade legislation—that fairly direct negotiations between American textile interests and the Japanese government (e.g., influencing the Japanese through what amounted, directly or indirectly, to Tokyo representation) played a part in getting Japan to agree to some sort of "voluntary quota." It seemed, too, to be the case, although I did not get any hard evidence on it, that Southern Maryland tobacco interests were not entirely passive in relationship to the Swiss government in efforts to discourage the watch industry from getting barriers erected against Swiss watches (the point being that Southern Maryland tobacco was supposed to have a better market in Switzerland than in the United States).

And, in the complex, interdependent, world of today, all sorts of pieces of "domestic" legislation are or can be affected by what happens in some foreign country. Usually, the effect is secondary and peripheral; but there are instances in which what is done abroad can have a considerable effect on what happens here. Labor legislation (because of costs), tax legislation (affecting mobile professionals such as movie stars), conservation of whales, legislation involving the control of epidemic diseases (whether of people or animals or plants), copyright law, antitrust policy, all are in point. Were I engaged in government relations for anybody concerned with these matters, I would like to know what is happening in other major capitals.

The U.N. and its affiliated organizations are more obvious. Judicial notice has been taken in this and other countries of U.N. policies and declarations. Some strength is probably lent to the planned parenthood movement in this country by the publicity given the support of planned parenthood by many members of the U.N. John D. Rockefeller III was probably more wisely employed in lobbying the U.N. delegations on this matter than he would have been in lobbying Congress or doing something else in Washington. Etc., etc., etc.

III.

Obviously, government relations can include a large portion of the world.

This has been partially true for a long time. For instance, it has always been the case that those who wished to influence government sometimes could achieve their objectives indirectly.

But the job of government relations is more far-reaching and inclusive nowadays for three major reasons:

1. Society—national and international—has grown more interdependent; there are more crossings of influence.

2. Side by side with the actual growth of interdependence has come the increasing awareness of interdependences. One of the great consequences of the social science way of thinking—a consequence which has influenced most professional men—is this awareness. Benjamin Franklin, as a London representative of the colony of Pennsylvania (carrying on in some ways exactly the same type of job that Washington representatives of the Governors of Alabama or Mississippi may now carry on) because he was a shrewd observer and an astute politician, was aware of many interdependences. But he, of course, lacked some of the facilities which a modern Washington representative possesses to find out about how specific interdependences relate to his problem; and he would have been even more ahead of his times than he was if he had had the viewpoint which would have enabled him to look at his job as involving the kind of approach here suggested.

3. And finally—partly due to the increasing complexity of

society and partly because so many more matters are seen[9] as subject to political handling than was the case a century ago—a far larger proportion of political decisions are made outside the Congress. It is not that Congress does less; it does more. But the increase in the total volume of political decisions has been so great that *proportionally* it does less. So, the notion of a Washington representative as a "lobbyist"—one who prowls the halls of Congress—whatever may have been its accuracy eighty years ago, is now outdated. Some matters, Congress has explicitly delegated to other agencies. In other cases, Congress has by inaction permitted other agencies to assume responsibilities for policymaking. And, in some instances, the growth of great national organizations has created new ways of achieving policy results, ways which involve bypassing Congress and making arrangements directly with executive agencies.

Government relations and Washington representation as a whole are a part of these newer political processes. Washington representatives negotiate and influence the outcome. The new, complex, responsible, diversified policy-making, means they sometimes speak for their constituencies, their principals, much as congressmen do, with a mixture of responsibility to the constituency and opportunity to use their own judgment similar to that which characterizes congressmen.[10] Washington representa-

---

[9] "Seen" is the deliberately chosen verb here. Decisions affecting business, churches, etc., in the late nineteenth century often were in fact closely tied up with politics and the government (often, of course, state governments, rather than the Washington government). But they were not "seen" or interpreted as such—for Rockefeller or Carnegie, *et al.*, to admit openly that, of necessity, they were involved with government and politics appeared corrupt or wrong-headed. Nowadays, most people realize that the different institutions of a society are necessarily interdependent. So, Washington representation and government relations can be carried on more professionally rather than in a seemingly underhand fashion.

[10] On this general issue see L. A. Dexter, "The Representative and His District," Bobbs-Merrill reprint PS-63 (also to appear in revised form in R. Peabody and N. Polsby, *New Perspectives on Congress* (Chicago: Rand McNally, 2nd ed. forthcoming, 1968–1969).

tives, that is, are becoming truly, political representatives, not mere agents—with the obligation which Edmund Burke emphasized to the electors of Bristol, "to serve your *interests*, not your *demands*." And the logic of the situation will drive clients and employers more and more to trust to the judgment of the representative, rather than simply to give him binding instructions.

4

WHEN THE JOB
IS CHIEFLY LOBBYING

A theme of this book is, "It isn't just lobbying." But, for some Washington representatives, the main job *is* lobbying; and for others at some times and periods, lobbying is major. This chapter covers (1) some sorts of situations when lobbying is or ought to be the procedure of choice in government relations; (2) considerations which effective lobbyists keep in mind—for instance, how to talk with congressmen and the emphasis on the soft sell; and (3) some *illustrations* of the technique of lobbying—such as "feeding questions" and establishing a legislative history.

Another topic which is suggested by the chapter is (4) that it is always worthwhile to look out and see whether lobbying may be counter-productive or wasteful. Much of it is one or the other.

I.

Lobbying is the choice when:

a. there is a reasonable likelihood that the Congress will take action which affects policy in the preferred direction; and

b. when there are enough resources available to the organization so that it can afford to invest time, energy, money, and good will in lobbying; and

c. when lobbying or its results do *not* run a great risk of becoming counterproductive.

I use the general phrase "take action," rather than the more specific "legislate," in order to include all the areas on which lobbyists might wish to approach congressmen or congressional employees. In the working vocabulary of American legislatures, legislation applies to statutes of a certain generality, but not always to appropriations, investigations, etc. But "nonlegislative" actions of Congress do in fact affect general policy. For instance, an investigation—sometimes even the threat of an investigation —can change, reinforce, or influence practices almost as much as a law. For instance, it appears that the real effect of the Kefauver, Humphrey, and Fountain investigations of pharmaceutical practices was not predominantly on specific legislation. Rather, they influenced relevant agencies—and also pharmaceutical companies[1]—to change policies. So, too, the investigations directed by Senator Joseph McCarthy had a considerable effect for some years on the treatment of male homosexuals in government and working on defense contracts, and perhaps in the entire society.

Equally clear and even more far-reaching is the effect of

---

[1] See Morton Mintz, *By Prescription Only* (Boston: Little, Brown, 1967).

appropriations and funding on policy.[2] If the Congress increases or cuts money, it may affect policy. A notable example of where policy was influenced through the appropriations process was provided by the House Subcommittee concerned with health budgets, under the late Representative John Fogarty. It consistently raised appropriations for Health Institutes beyond presidential requests, often accompanying a raise with a directive.

And confirmation of appointments—or failure to confirm them—certainly may have an effect on policy. Any systematic emphasis by several senators on the kinds of appointments they will disapprove, or on the kinds of patronage they will demand, could influence policy. After all, men influence measures.[3]

In order to find out whether there is a reasonable prospect of the Congress's taking action in some preferred direction, a lobbyist needs to have accurate information about the committees, the leadership, and the schedule, and, of course, about demands from the executive branch, influential groups in the country, and constituencies. A great many bills are introduced

[2] See Richard Fenno, *Power of the Purse: Appropriation Politics in Congress* (Boston: Little, Brown, 1966).

[3] It is said that the late Senator McCarran had considerable influence over the Immigration and Naturalization Service, and other units in the Department of Justice, precisely because he was able as a sort of patronage to determine middle-level appointments as well as some at higher levels. It does not matter, for our present purposes, whether this was true or not. The point is that it could be true of any able, aggressive, astute senator, over a period of years (and probably also of a senior House member). In a sense, of course, helping or persuading a senator or congressman to use such influence is not "lobbying" but "congressional interference in administration," to use Kenneth Gray's term. Also, the Senate does have a definite, constitutional responsibility for confirming judicial appointments; and it seems almost certain that the influence of several southern senators during the Kennedy administration did tend to discourage the appointment of circuit and district judges who might have quickly implemented the Supreme Court's position on civil rights—not even so much by holding up or insisting on specific appointments, but because, when calculating the chances for potential nominees, the administration itself ruled out those who would run into real trouble with the Judiciary Committee of the Senate, which must first approve nominations to judgeships, and which has several southern members.

each year. The Washington representative who can afford the time will keep track of any which may be relevant. He should find out why the member who introduced them did so; and he will see if anything can usefully be said, *and by whom,* to the member or to the people at whose request the bill was introduced.

A great many bills are *introduced* each year—but few are *chosen* for serious consideration by a committee. Limitations on time and attention mean that only a few measures can be considered by a given committee in a given session. Accordingly, if the preferences of the *active* members of the committee are known, if the priorities of the executive departments are evident, and if some reflection is given to what is likely to be urged from outside the Congress or by the leadership and referred to a given committee,[4] the schedule for a particular year can be more or less foreseen. Since most measures which are introduced will not be taken up seriously in committee, there is little reason to do a great deal about them, unless:

a. Organizing sentiment for them serves to publicize the proposal (or its dangerousness) and make one's supporters enthusiastic. A good many measures have been introduced chiefly in the hope of such publicity, even though there is little or no prospect of enactment or even committee consideration.

b. Trying to do something about them serves as a way to get congressmen and staffs to pay attention to a problem and a

---

[4] With very rare exceptions, any measure will have to be considered by a committee before it goes to the floor of the Congress. There is some leeway—but not by any means an unlimited amount—in determining which measure goes to which committee. Knowledge of history and procedure helps to determine when such leeway exists; emphasis and key words can be juggled in order to lead to reference to committee X rather than committee Y—or, occasionally, with subcommittees who are sympathetic, some of the purposes of legislation may be achieved by recasting a proposed policy change in terms of a resolution so that it leads to an investigation; or some actions may be initiated without going to the floor in the committee. On all such matters, see Bertram Gross, *The Legislative Struggle* (New York: McGraw-Hill, 1953).

proposal—so that in some future year, even if not in this one, they might take up the matter seriously.

There is a third reason why it makes sense for some Washington representatives to do something about proposals that have only a slight chance of being enacted, although such activities do not help the "cause":

c. Activity—introducing a measure, sending out the alarm about another, and so on—may make some clients and supporters feel that the Washington representative really is doing something, that he's on the ball, that there is need to keep him there. "Going through the motions"—as part of what sociologists call "maintenance functions"—is a large part of all politics—for that matter, of most work. To the extent that an organization relies upon the support of what may be called unsophisticated consumers, no doubt a Washington representative has to engage in this sort of make-believe. There have been, for instance, occasions when a bill or resolution was introduced by a member, when both he and the lobbyist who wrote it knew for certain that it would never get anywhere. A cheap way for a congressman to do a favor for a lobbyist is to introduce such a bill; it gives the lobbyist a talking point with his "constituents," members of his organization. *And congressmen, who after all must spend a lot of time "going through the motions" for electoral purposes, deeply sympathize.*

For a group like the prewar National Council for the Prevention of War (Fred Libby, Jeanette Rankin, *et al.*), the introduction of hopeless measures could be a consequence of the politically unsophisticated character of their support—and also of their own feeling that they must push forward hard for the cause, regardless of practicalities. But a sophisticated government relations program—one run by a business firm or on behalf of most professional associations—presumably will minimize mere gestures. An astute client will certainly want to find out whether his Washington representative really has calculated the score and is best employed in pushing for hopeless measures. Of course, there are times when a Washington representative would never himself introduce a given measure; but some of his allies do so, and in order not to lose their cooperation he has to do something in a battle which he knows can never be won. You can protect yourself, perhaps, from your enemies; *but* your friends inevitably waste your time.

II.

The important consideration, of course, is what alternative courses of nonlobbying action are open to the Washington representative which may further the organization's cause—where the chances of success are better. He must also know accurately what resources he has! One of the general statements that can be made most emphatically about Washington representation is this: Most creative and imaginative Washington representatives do not have nearly enough resources to do all that might be conceived of. There are just too many access routes, too many ways in which the Federal government impinges or could impinge upon the organization.

Bauer, Pool, and I concluded in our 1953–1955 analysis of the reciprocal trade controversy and of the lobbyists on both sides of that issue:

> One saw only harassed men with tight budgets and limited campaign funds, once their essential organizational overheads had been met. . . . In working for any legislative cause, there is just too much to do. For instance, an executive of a trade association has to concern himself not only with national policies but finances, membership, meetings, bulletins, magazines, correspondence, inquiries, staffing. . . . He must follow legislative and administrative developments, not only on tariffs but also on government contracts, taxes, and regula-

tions of different sorts. He has also to collect economic statistics, business and scientific and legislative reports.

If he is in a single issue organization, such as the Committee on a National Trade Policy or the Strackbein ("protectionist") Committee, he is concerned with changes in tariff rates and regulations for each of the products listed in the tariff rules. He is concerned, not only with the Reciprocal Trade Bill and all its ramifications, but also with customs simplification, GATT (General Agreement on Trade and Tariffs), OTC (Organization for Trade Cooperation), Buy-American legislation, agricultural legislation (much of which was related to export policy, but did not fall within the Reciprocal Trade statute) and such proceedings as Tariff Commission escape clause proceedings and State Department reciprocal-trade negotiations.

In this day of big government, there is never enough time to do more than select from among its complexities what to cope with, or else to drift, pushed by events into a few of the many things one might do.

We added, "Most pressure group activity is emergency fire fighting. There is seldom time to do much more. Long range planning goes by default."[5] As a report on the activities of the reciprocal trade lobbyists of 1953–1955, this statement is correct. But it need not be true inevitably and always.

And, in fact, the Washington representative who reacts— or is typically forced by his client to react—to some congressional proposal without determining priorities ends up by being even less effective than the semiprepared emergency fire-fighter of our metaphor. He resembles more nearly a mother who spends hours bandaging a child's minor cuts when both that child and her

[5] From R. Bauer, I. Pool, and L. Dexter, *American Business and Public Policy* (New York: Atherton, 1963), pp. 345, 348–349. I have made a few minor modifications in quoting; quotation by permission.

other children have major unanswered needs and illnesses. Here, as in most other professional matters, the balancing of priorities is necessary to long-range effective action, and here as in many professions, the balancing of priorities is in fact probably exceptional. Nevertheless it should be attempted.

III.

Probably, in terms of total manpower—certainly in terms of total *business* lobbying manpower—most lobbying is "defensive." That is, when some legislative proposal threatens to upset the established order, then lobbyists, professional and amateur, descend on Capitol Hill. This is natural enough; it is much easier to get successful people (the kind who finance and initiate most lobbies) excited about having a favorable situation disturbed than to stir them up (at least in American society) about a contingent benefit.

It has often, although not always, tended since 1933 to be the case that the administration has proposed changes which would disturb some established interest. So, then, established interests have looked to the Congress to prevent the change or modify its harmful effects on them. Consequently, in Congress, to some extent, among lobbyists to a very great degree, the defensive point of view is common.

The generally more conservative cast of Congress, at least on economic matters, means that it often is the last, best hope of endangered interests. More often than not, to be sure, the damage feared by some interest is not so great as apprehensions suggest; and/or the rhetoric about the threat is vastly exaggerated. (Think, for instance, of generally respectable and even "liberal" congressmen, who preached in 1954 that a minor expansion of reciprocal trade was the product of the Communist conspiracy, first hatched by Harry Dexter White, in order to undermine the whole economic strength of the United States!)

Such exaggerations often inhibit discussion of administrative routes and mechanisms by which damage can be avoided. It is quite possible that, if medical interests had tried to prevent some of the real administrative difficulties Medicare and Medicaid would create for them, they could have done so; but the focus of attention was such that administrative considerations could only be really entered into after the legislation was put into effect. Rhetoric obscured consideration of reality. Right now, one of the arguments—which sounds valid—of some pharmaceutical firms against the careful testing now demanded by Federal agencies for new drugs, is that this slows down dreadfully the introduction of drugs which are essential for some people's lives or comfort. But, if this really is true, there are obvious enough administrative ways of making the harm less serious than it would be without planning.

Now, of course, no one should expect an endangered interest to admit that there are ways of modifying the dangers it fears, so long as it believes it can win an all-out victory. But a careful assessment of situations by the government relations department certainly should suggest possibilities of and reactions to partial defeat. I have been told that one of the big auto companies was pretty sure in advance it could live with most auto safety legislation and regulations (bitterly as it resisted them) because it felt it could establish a working relationship with any possible administrator. In this case, the company had probably thought through how much additional investment of effort was justified in fighting the whole movement.

IV.

Most lobbyists, most of the time, act to reenforce, strengthen, aid, and reassure congressmen and staff who tend to be on their side. They relatively rarely *argue* with known enemies.

This, in general, is sensible enough. Most senators, congressmen, and staff "on our side" on the issue nevertheless need to be reminded frequently. They have many other interests, *priorities*, and concerns. Indeed, the amazing thing to anyone who comes from an environment where some particular issue is really important—be it what it may—and who talks with a dozen people on Capitol Hill, is to learn how unimportant that issue seems to most of them. I who knew all this, nevertheless, in November 1967, was surprised by it over Vietnam—how much less crucial to congressional staff than to most people I personally knew! (Of course, I myself felt it very strongly!) It is not that congressmen and staff are callous or indifferent or lacking in public spirit. It is rather that, on the one hand, they are so public spirited about so many things, that they do not possess the emotional energy to be as involved in any one or two things as most people. And, they are what T. V. Smith called in his little book on *The Legislative Way of Life* "brokers of consciences" so they cannot afford absolute priorities. And, of course, although "in sympathy" on some particular matter, the matter may be one of very slight significance to them, although, of course, of high priority to someone. For example, they may be simply speaking for a constituency concern, which seems to them respectable, but which, were they private citizens, they would not lift a finger for.

Aside from reminding people, lobbyists can and do help friends by supplying information, feeding useful questions, writing speeches, making analyses of reports, finding out who is lined up how on any matter of concern—generally making themselves useful, whenever they can. Frequently, the speeches or the reports are rather unrelated to the lobbyist's own mission. The point is, to a considerable degree, to aid the friend; if he is the sort of man who reciprocates, this creates a sense of obligation, and also makes it likely that the lobbyist will be consulted on something of relevance to his own mission. But this sort of helpfulness uses up the lobbyist's scarcest resource—time! One reason, I suspect, why a few lobbyists close their minds to other aspects of being a Washington representative is that if they pursued them they would no longer be able to help congressmen and senators as much—and they enjoy being in effect auxiliary staff members.

The professional image which most of the lobbyists I have known personally hold is: "You must always be straightforward with congressmen and senators." From half-a-dozen different lobbyists, I have independently heard the story of how so-and-so on the Hill asked them about such-and-such a measure, and after studying it, the comment was: "Now, of course, in terms of my organization, I wish you'd do thus-and-so. But, in fact, in terms of your relationship to (your district) (your record) (your contributors) (your colleagues or committee) you ought to do the reverse." And this story is concluded: "I always play fair with them. I never try to fool them." Similarly, speeches are said to be prepared, etc., in terms of what the congressman can safely say, not what the lobbyist favors. And the congressman allegedly is not pushed into things that would create trouble—for him! Or, if he is, the trouble is explained.

I doubt whether practice is always this uninvolved, but it is significant that the image has developed widely, and independently. A lobbyist must be trusted by congressmen and senators (and furthermore he cherishes the feeling they trust him because perhaps he rarely can find clients, newspapermen, or friends, who have a correct appreciation of what he does!)

If he has to choose, certainly, a lobbyist is better off to mislead or deceive his client(s) than to deceive or mislead important or talkative congressmen. I suppose the same thing is generally true of attorneys with a lot of courtroom business; they are better off to mislead most clients as to procedure than to mislead sophisticated judges or fellow-attorneys. For if a judge or a fellow-attorney, in the one instance, a congressman or a committee clerk in the other, is deceived, it is likely to have long-range effects—and, in our case, it is likely to become known to many other people on Capitol Hill. In this very connection, two of the

Washington representatives who told me about their straight-forwardness with congressmen told, at other times, of ways in which they had in fact misled clients. In one case, campaign contributions were collected for a member of Congress, whom both the lobbyist and I admire, on the ground that he would help the clients' interests (when both the lobbyist and I knew this to be highly improbable). The lobbyist was rather pleased with his shrewdness, I thought, as he recollected how he had diverted campaign funds "in the public interest."

As a result of the general ethical emphasis on discretion on Capitol Hill, respected not only by lobbyists but by journalists, congressmen are extraordinarily open with informed people who come in and talk to them. Books like *American Business and Public Policy*, and numerous other studies of Congress, are possible because congressmen have this kind of frankness and openness, which they carry over to scholars. They will say very freely: "I don't want to do this, but Y (a colleague) felt I'd be letting him down, if I didn't." "Of course, the proposal is quite wrong, but I'm tied up by obligations to such-and-such a (constituency interest) (campaign contributor)." And they expect that this will be treated as off-the- record, background stuff. Everyone understands it will not be published or repeated to people too unsophisticated to understand the complex web of obligations within which any statesman operates. Partly, too, it operates, I think, because so much congressional discussion with lobbyists, legislative liaison people, and the like is conducted in terms of: "I'd like to go along with you, but here are practical reasons why I can't. See, I really am a good fellow!"

V.

Lobbying known opponents or the indifferent is a more difficult and less rewarding thing, by far, than lobbying friends or potential friends.

I was surprised in my early contacts with Capitol Hill to hear several different legislative assistants in the Senate comment on the unwillingness of interest group representatives to come in and see them. "It's shocking," declared one senator's executive secretary. "I used to be a lobbyist myself; and I simply can't understand it. They just don't come in and see us; and they should. We might listen to them; and there are a lot of things we don't know about." And, the late Sam Jacobs, when he was, in effect, legislative assistant to Senator McNamara of Michigan, complained about the failure, as he saw it, of (1) representatives of some union groups and (2) representatives of certain mental health groups to come in and see him or his colleagues. "We want to hear from them. . . ." "Yes," he said in an answer to a comment, "I can understand why [the labor groups in question] don't come to see us." [Sam had been a lobbyist for the UAW; McNamara had for many years been a leader of the Pipefitters, and the union people who didn't come in and see him or the Senator, represented a third union which I believe had had frictions with both these unions.] "But they could throw their hats in, and see what happened . . . I just don't understand it." As I now recollect, he spoke of several fruitless attempts to get lobbyists for the mental health groups to come in and see him or the Senator; my impression was that he felt that these groups regarded the Senator as an uneducated, old-style labor type, not worth serious bother, and was hurt by the implied slight.

I have known of several occasions where, it seemed to me, newly elected congressmen or newly appointed executive assistants felt themselves in a vacuum. They had thought they were going to be besieged by lobbyists, pressure groups, interests. And, instead, they hardly heard from any except those to which they were already committed.[6]

---

[6] Of course, one reason for this is that, due to the seniority system on committees, junior, new members, usually matter far less than older ones.

For some years, my reaction to this situation was that, clearly, this showed the human tendency to take the easy path. Lobbyists, like most of us, do not like to face hostility—so, I said, they take the easy way out. I still think that there is an important element of that in the situation. But, nevertheless, there is an important argument against lobbying the hostile or the uncommitted.

It runs like this: The chief effect of publicity, propaganda, and public relations is to focus attention on a problem. Quite frequently, publicity by advocates of a cause: (1) has alerted opponents, stimulated them to the feeling that something ought to be done, made them more apt to act against the cause, or (2) has led people who were neutral about the issue to realize that in terms of their basic values they are against the position advocated. Certainly, our impression in our study of reciprocal trade was that the communications, publicity, pressure, and hullaballoo, "act on people more as triggers than forces. . . . [For instance] League of Women Voters propaganda [might under quite probable specified circumstances] have the effect of activating a larger number of . . . protectionists than of . . . free traders."[7]

Now, a lobbyist who calls on a hostile or uncommitted congressman may have exactly this effect: his lobbying may be

---

But the time to convince or influence genuinely uncommitted members, or simply to establish a favorable relationship with them, is when they have leisure—perhaps the middle of their first session, after they have adapted and come to realize that in Washington they are not such big items, after all. Who knows—if they stay—what committees they will be transferred to or how much seniority they will achieve? Of course, a lot of them will not be reelected, but, some of them can become crucial. It is a worthwhile investment.

I am speaking, here, as of the 1950's, when I spent more time in congressional offices; perhaps, this particular situation has changed in the 1960's and first-termers are not as ignored.

[7] See Bauer, Pool, and Dexter, *American Business and Public Policy*, pp. 466ff. A similar approach to the issue is argued by E. E. Schattschneider, *The Semi-Sovereign People* (New York: Holt, Rinehart, and Winston, 1961). He interprets the issue, however, in terms of the theory of organizational crowd behavior; whereas we tackled it in terms of communications theory and arrived at the same conclusion.

counterproductive. In some instances, it most emphatically is, because it leads hostile congressmen to threaten an investigation of lobbying or of the particular lobby group. But, if lobbyists really have thought this through, why do they encourage all manner of constituents to write to congressmen who are known to be hostile?

SALESMEN OR MISSIONARIES.

It is of some interest that I got the clear impression from interviews on Capitol Hill in the 1950's that two lobbying groups were then particularly unpopular, even with quite liberal congressmen. These were the CIO unions and the League of Women Voters.[8] Now, these are among the lobbyists who do not leave opponents alone—who have a mission and follow through on it. Perhaps, their unpopularity was due just to this reason. On the other hand, there is no hard evidence that being unpopular means being ineffective; perhaps, a certain amount can be accomplished when one becomes unpopular, but since lobbying should be a continuing, rather than a transient relationship, wearing out one's welcome presumably is dangerous.

The problem is, granted a limited number of possible people to influence, should lobbyists take the standpoint of the salesmen who follow through on the good prospects but quickly abandon any effort to influence the unpromising ones—or should they imitate missionaries, eager to convert the unrighteous and hard of heart, as well as the malleable and persuadable? This is a problem which, in many forms, faces many of us frequently— which, for instance, should teachers do—imitate missionaries or salesmen?

In any event, in the 1960's I have been concerned, also, with

[8] See Bauer, Pool, and Dexter, *American Business and Public Policy*, "The Ladies of the League," Chap. 27.

lobbying in state capitals. And I have asked state legislators: What are the most unpopular lobbying groups? The answer has been, flatly, for at least ten different states, "Teacher groups *and* union representatives."

The conclusion seems obvious enough. But there are other factors:

1. Unions and Leagues of Women Voters usually have a *program*, rather than simply a few issues. Quite probably, what wearies congressmen and state legislators is listening to a whole program—certainly that is a complaint. "They just cover so damn much; and they tell you all about it." Whereas a more typical lobbyist, with a narrower set of issues, can and does ask for help and advice.

2. It may also be a matter of how the approach is made, how the interview is conducted by the lobbyist. A lobbyist ought to be able entirely to divorce himself from the role of missionary and say in a believable fashion (by his manner, if not in words): "Look, I'm here to exchange views with you. Later on, my associates or I will, of course, try to influence you. But, before I talk with you, I want to know your position, what you want, how you feel about things in our field, and why you feel that way. If you're for us, good, maybe we can help each other; if you are against us, I want to know why—maybe there are, even so, some things we have in common; if you are in doubt, or think the whole issue a bore, I'd like to know why, too." This is, in essence, good interviewing, and,[9] as I understand it, especially in relation to capital goods, good salesmanship.

I suspect that lobbyists who can adopt this approach are productive, on the average, with opponents or neutrals particularly to the extent that they adopt the vocabulary and point of

[9] See Lewis A. Dexter, *Elite and Specialized Interviewing* (possibly to be retitled), (Chicago: Markham Publishing Co., 1969), forthcoming.

view of the latter while talking with them.[10] Then, on the basis of such *information-getting* efforts (and note this *is* information getting) they can tell what is worth following up. They will certainly find out that some people who are supposed to be hostile are not so at all. It is a constant phenomenon on Capitol Hill that someone whom "everybody knows" is against a given position turns out to favor it. People infer from general reputation, idle comments of a few years ago, associations, imperfect knowledge of friendships and alliances, and they make mistakes.

VI.

Concentration on lobbying is called for most clearly when the executive department is almost uniformly hostile and when there is some access to the Congress.

Three examples of this situation: *First,* at present, all-out opponents of the Vietnam War have little to hope for from the executive department. There is no information which they can get from the executive about developments in Vietnam which is particularly useful. There is little value in exchange of views between, say, the State Department and SANE. There may be, hopefully, a change in either or both these regards, so it is desirable to keep up any marginal contacts which are possible (on such matters as nuclear disarmament, which is also of interest to most opponents of the Vietnam War). But on their main issue, opponents of the Vietnam War are outside the executive "consensus."

However, factors which make it likely that they cannot do much with the executive branch mean that they can do something in the way of Capitol Hill lobbying. Most of the time, on

---

[10] See Lewis A. Dexter "Role Relationships and Conceptions of Neutrality in Interviewing," *American Journal of Sociology*, 62 (1956) 153–157.

many issues, many members of Congress feel (often correctly) that they can get honest, aboveboard, information from the numerous specialists in the executive departments. But, in regard to the Vietnam War, this is regarded as less certain.

And yet, there are many members of the Congress who have real doubts—who want ideas and suggestions—as to the Vietnam War. It is, probably, true that the "Vietnik" approach and stereotype does not provide a particularly good introduction on Capitol Hill, but, nevertheless, some hesitating members will listen—and the more the message is presented in moderate, middle-class terms, the more they will listen. Probably, members would be more receptive to the kind of opposition expressed by General Shoup or Walter Lippmann than by the standard peace groups, but even the "Vietniks" will be heeded.

Then, too, there are congressmen who want to keep an anchor out to windward; it is clear, for instance, that the Kennedy brothers had excellent reasons to pay some attention to the opponents of the Vietnam War. And so does Senator Percy.

But the biggest lobbying service of opponents of the Vietnam War should be, as has already been discussed, what lobbyists generally do best—reenforcing, providing ammunition for, and serving their sympathizers in the Congress."[11]

A *second* instance where lobbying is clearly the best route is provided by the chiropractic associations. They are interested in getting equality of treatment in health programs, in the Department of Defense, in Selective Service, and of course in edu-

---

[11] It is, of course, quite possible in the Vietnam case and in the two following cases that something might be done through the states, through the courts, through international action. In fact, on Vietnam, a good deal is happening (whether through any kind of coordinated planning or not I do not know), e.g., in Canada and Sweden which may have some effects on American policy. There are also (written, November 1967) possibilities of court action later: the trial of Dr. Spock for conspiracy may give an example here. Evidently, the newspapers have been the best allies of the Vietniks.

cational grants and aids, so far as their own medical colleges go. Generally speaking, for them to try to get anything from the executive departments is what one of their advocates calls "a very rough hustle." The medical orthodoxy of administrators and physicians in the government service is unbreachable.

But there are members of Congress who are sympathetic, either because of personal feelings or because in home districts chiropractors are fervently believed in. (There is great regional variation, apparently, in the support of chiropractic; it is much stronger in the interior than on the East Coast, for instance). Congressmen can force some bureaucrats to take note of the powerful feeling behind the cause. They could also, on some specific matters, require by legislation grants and aids and opportunities be extended on an equal basis with medical doctors.

A *third* example where Congress is a better bet than the bureaucracy is the National Health Foundation. Its mission is the preservation of what it regards as the basic nutritional character of foods against the harmful effects of adulterants, preservatives, chemicals, etc. It has, in fact, in some instances according to its interpretation of the facts, played a part in getting Federal agencies to begin to accept its arguments. It is likely that congressional introductions and concerns assisted in these victories. The point of view is sufficiently persuasive so that it could well influence some legislation; it is far more likely to have such an influence on Capitol Hill than downtown. For downtown, in the relevant bureaus, its views are heresy—or dangerous.

Another kind of situation where lobbying is definitely the choice: continuous newspaper coverage and related publicity can be secured by a dramatic congressional investigation. The Kefauver investigation of the drug industry did indeed put some matters on the front pages and led influential people to be aware of them. (Interestingly enough, however, the Humphrey and Fountain investigations of the same subject did not receive nearly as much national attention). It alerted people to what might happen; and when it did happen, in the case of the birth-defect babies, considerable change in policy, both legislatively and in the administration, took place.

In principle, of course, the executive departments or the regulatory commissions might hold equally dramatic hearings. But the tradition of Congress, and its institutional organization, probably make it easier to arrange for drama there. Of course, many investigations are not particularly dramatic; and some, dramatic or not, lead nowhere. Earlier Kefauver investigations—for instance, that on civil defense—did not accomplish a great deal in terms of policy change. For Kefauver's particular style —which was one of alerting people—they did not work out.

The classic example of investigations which do have a legislative effect is perhaps what is called the Nye investigation—the studies of the munitions trade in the 1930's. And, in this case, it seems that Dorothy Detzer of the Women's International League for Peace and Freedom, and other lobbyists, planned it that way. The legislative results had no necessary logical connection with the facts unearthed in the hearings; but they did fit into the objectives of the lobbyists who had stimulated the investigation to begin with.

There are also investigations which do not receive any great coverage in the mass media but which do have an effect on professionals and experts. The massive studies by the Tolman Subcommittee some twenty-five years ago of migrant workers and their problems had, probably, a lasting effect in creating general attitudes on this topic. I suspect that in the long run the Humphrey-Fountain investigations of the pharmaceutical industry will prove similarly influential.

I do not know whether any of these investigations were in fact stimulated by lobbyists; but they could have been.

Of course, most of the time, the typical lobbyist is not going to be able to find a congressman or senator who can and will undertake a desired sort of investigation. But, over the course of any given session, a good many lobbyists may be able to influence who is called, what is said, and perhaps the nuances of what is reported in a relevant investigation. Basically, this can only be done by those who are willing to look at matters from the investigator's point of view. DuPont, once Senator Nye and associates had gotten really under way, had no hope of seriously altering the direction of the munitions investigation. But it could, once it accepted Nye's general objectives and point of view, perhaps have indicated ways in which it would be cooperative, which would lead away from legislative results it might deplore. And those ways should have been suggested in terms of Nye's interest in national publicity, publicity back home, and the like.

It might have been theoretically possible for the pharmaceutical industry to exert influence which would have led to killing the Humphrey or Fountain investigations. But it would have been dangerous to push such an effort, because, if found out, nothing would have been more sure to put the whole business on the front pages. But what the industry, to some extent, as a whole, might have done would be to try to think of "red herrings," matters which would attract the investigators, probably help to determine the report, but not lead in any dangerous directions.

Evidently, this is a situation where individual firms might have competing interests. If Firm X has abandoned some practice which others in the industry still follow of a sort which might worry the investigators, of course, it would be helpful to have attention called to this. But, since Firm X has to continue to live with its industry colleagues, that would be a tricky effort. Or Firm X may have taken unusual precautions against harmful side-effects of the drugs which it manufactures, which it can call to attention, perhaps by feeding questions to a sympathetic member of the committee.

We have been talking here about two cases where the lobbying effort would have been in fact defensive, DuPont in the 1930's, the pharmaceutical industry in the 1960's. But, it is of course possible to introduce matters which are more or less irrelevant to the original conception of the investigation. For instance, in principal it would have been possible to use the Humphrey-Fountain investigations to spread fear of "the pill" and weaken birth control sentiment, if there were lobbyists around with that objective. Or, if any member of the committee had been at all sympathetic, these investigations might have been used to strike a small blow for the cause of the National Health Foundation, by stressing the idea that all drugs are dangerous (iatrogenic) for the same sorts of reasons that additives are dangerous in ordinary food.

As a practical matter, most congressmen and staff, even as you and I, cannot take the time to plow through mountains of testimony; unlike some of us, they may read committee reports, but on a day-to-day basis what they know about an investigation in committees other than their own they learn from the newspapers and news magazines. Consequently, any lobbyist might find it helpful to have testimony in hearings *interpreted* by the news media in relationship to his cause, even if the testimony itself did not introduce the relationship. Quite conceivably, for instance, some columnist or reporter might be persuaded to point out implications of testimony about the dangerousness of drugs so as to suggest the dangerousness of food additives.

VII.

In the nature of the case, committee members often welcome suggestions as to questions to ask witnesses. Members have a multitude of responsibilities. Witnesses are better briefed and prepared than is a committee member who, perhaps, belongs to a dozen other subcommittees.

Committee members, in general, have an attitude and orientation of "probing," of "challenging." They tend to feel that there is an issue on which they can pass judgment when witnesses contradict each other, when the facts adduced by different witnesses are in conflict, etc. The model in their minds is often that of adversary proceedings in the law—the dominant influence in Congress, of course, is that of lawyers.[12] So, searching questions, especially for witnesses, regarded with some suspicion, are welcomed, because the staff will be casting around for questions to ask. Naturally, if anyone is regarded as trustworthy or even competent, he has, under such circumstances, a chance to "feed" questions to the senator or congressman. Naturally, too, a stranger or one who is not trusted, will not have as many opportunities to suggest questions. Obviously, too, familiarity with the preferences of a particular interrogator or his staff, or with the kind of press coverage a particular investigation is getting makes a difference as to how effective a lobbyist can be along this line.

VIII.

It would be possible to continue the discussion of committee questioning at considerable length. What sort of questions get asked why? What sort of biases does the committee system *as a system* impose upon the investigator, the would-be legislator, the lobbyist? But to consider these matters adequately would demand far more knowledge than I possess. I hope that some one will study the whole process of questioning, hearings and testimony, in sociological and political terms—not only with relation to legislative committees, but in regard to appropriations, in regard to Royal Commissions in Canada, in regard to quasi-

---

12 For a discussion of this model in Congress, see L. A. Dexter, "Congressmen and the Formulation of Military Policy" in R. Peabody & N. Polsby, *New Perspectives on Congress*, (Chicago: Rand McNally, 1963 [2nd ed. forthcoming, 1969]).

regulatory agencies here. Such an effort would get far beyond the scope of this book, however.

There is another area of importance where an effective lobbyist can have great impact. That is in establishing a clear "legislative history" favorable to his interest. In the nature of the case, laws always have to be interpreted and administered. They are interpreted and administered, supposedly, in terms of "the intent of the Congress." The courts, and the executive agencies, try to ascertain that intent from discussion on the floor, committee reports, and anything else which is credible, authoritative, and relevant. Consequently, a skillful lobbyist will arrange —and some have arranged—to set up discussions on the floor, running something like this: An honorable member asks the floor manager of the bill or some other responsible committee member to explain certain points. "This bill," he may ask "is intended, is it not, to cover X, Y, Z, but not, of course Q?" And "It is not intended to change prevailing practice in regard to R?" These discussions are planned beforehand, perhaps with both sides being written by the lobbyist. The lobbyist—*if he also knows the bureaucracy and the courts*—will probably foresee better than most congressmen how these latter might interpret a given clause, in a way to help or hurt his clients and their interests. Talking with one man who had recently created a legislative history in this fashion, he emphasized: "But you see, I know the general counsel in the administering agency. I know we have to be very careful—we can't leave him any leeway to interpret it in such-and-such a way. It has to be put down in black and white, so he has no loophole left. And that's what we did." Another lobbyist in similar circumstances might have his eye on the courts. If a lobbyist has established sufficiently good rapport, he might have a chance to suggest language for the committee report or help in the speeches with which some members of the committee introduce a measure.

In general, a man will do better at this sort of work if he has had considerable knowledge of the relevant bureaus and/or the courts. For then, he will foresee what they may say, what they may do. But if his experience has been confined to Capitol Hill or to his own industry, he is less likely to think in the necessary terms. Obviously, some people on Capitol Hill, legislative assistants, men who do a lot of "casework" with a particular agency, learn a good deal about the bureaucracy. But, one often-heard judgment is relevant. In replying to the question "Who makes a good lobbyist?" several lobbyists said, without my raising the point, "Never an ex-congressman." I suspect a congressman who has only been a congressman, and has not had administrative or staff responsibility in Washington, does usually make a reasonably poor lobbyist, precisely because he does not foresee how the bureaus will interpret things—he does not dot the i's and cross the t's—committee clerks and assistants have always done that for him. And a congressman is probably much worse in one way than a man from industry. He thinks he knows the trade of lobbying, but he does not; the man from industry usually knows he has a lot to learn.

Both these rather specialized examples of lobbying skills—feeding questions, getting a helpful legislative history—clearly demand *information* about a number of bureaucratic and public relations matters, as well as about the internal workings of the Congress. Any other specialized instances of lobbying skill which might be chosen for discussion similarly demand, first and foremost, information. So, we come to the notion: *information is the commodity above all others which the lobbyist, like other Washington representatives, needs.* Pull, access, personality, are often regarded as fundamental to the effective lobbyist. They are helpful, sometimes necessary, as secondary resources. *But information and skill in its use without pull or access or "personality" to back it can in general secure access and influence; access and "personality" and pull, without the skilled use of information, rarely get effective, continuing influence!*

5

HELPING AND SEEKING HELP ON CAPITOL HILL

The Planning of Government Relations and Congressional Patterns in Favor-Handling

Even on Capitol Hill, the main job of Washington representatives is not lobbying as such. Rather, it is using Congress as a means of influencing the administrative branch or of getting information or of achieving favorable publicity for an organization.

Almost certainly, the great volume of what looks like lobbying and would be called lobbying in an ordinary news story is not. To the contrary, most contacts with congressmen and staff by petitioners are requests for help about personal, business, and professional problems with government.

I.

Handling such requests for professional, business, and personal help is called "case work." Many cases in the nature of the situation are submitted by people who otherwise function as genuine Washington representatives. This fact has a good deal of significance both for Washington representatives and for congressmen, and, indeed, for our whole system of government.

A Washington representative, for example, of a major hotel chain, might easily approach a friendly congressman in the course of a session on the following four matters:

a. asking for help in getting an amendment or a relevant legislative history to a revision of the Wages and Hours Act which will permit the hotel industry to handle overtime in hotel laundries on the same basis that it is handled for other hotel employees.[1]

b. asking for help in persuading relevant authorities in the Office of Education, the Treasury, and the Department of Commerce to provide special aids and grants for students "interning" as couriers or guides or receptionists for foreign visitors to the United States, in order to encourage European tourism in this country[2] and to train hotel personnel.

c. asking the congressman to use his influence in getting a particular national meeting under the auspices of a government

---

[1] The problem here—a real one—is that hotel employees, because of seasonal, etc., aspects of the business may be paid "straight time" whereas employees in ordinary laundries are paid time plus rates for overtime. When laundry employees are put under the coverage of overtime statutes and regulations, should hotel laundry workers be treated like hotel workers or laundry workers? Such decisions can affect costs noticeably.

[2] I do not know that any hotel or tourism interest has ever attempted anything of the sort—but in view of the current emphasis on increasing European tourism and business visits to the United States, a good argument could be advanced for it. It might be worth trying.

department, held at one of the chain's hotels, so as to publicize the hotel and the chain.

d. asking the congressman to help in getting the Selective Service System (perhaps through various government agencies which are believed to have an influence on the latter) to grant deferments to the sons of the major owner of the chain, who hold independent responsibilities in its management—on the ground that because of the numerous defense-related conferences held at the hotels, these young men are engaged in defense work of national importance.[3]

But, in fact, the first two requests, generally speaking, involve policy concerns; whereas the latter two would, ordinarily, be handled in terms of already existing policies. The first two are Washington representation; the second two, casework requests.

Of course, any one familiar with the tradition of Anglo-American law "slowly broadening down from precedent to precedent" knows that the line between routine-handling of a case and policy formation is not always clear. Also, it is possible to find legislators and executives like ex-Senator Paul Douglas of Illinois[4]—who purposefully look at cases to see if they suggest or raise policy issues. But Douglas' approach is uncommon, and, in fact, most of the cases which were processed by his office— even some of the most dramatic among them—were simply cases. The only policy aspect to them was that they showed the incredibly "stuffy" unwillingness of some bureaucrats to admit error or to abandon legalisms; that is to say, they showed that bureaucrats are "bureaucrats."[5] Most of the time, cases are simply

[3] I have never talked with a hotel chain executive or representative and do not assert any hotel chain has ever made efforts along this line, however, I do know that firms in other industries have made analogous efforts.

[4] See the description of Senator Douglas' handling of cases in a paper by Kenneth Gray, "Congressional Interference in Administration," in *Cooperation and Conflict*, ed. D. Elazar (Itasca: F. E. Peacock, 1969).

[5] See the account of one such case, the Buck case, placed in the Congressional Record by Senator Douglas on September 13, 1965. There were substantial further developments after this date.

cases, and the overlapping problem is merely a modification of the old logician's dilemma: How many hairs make a beard? Any experienced person intuitively knows 99 times out of 100 whether a given request is going to be handled in casework terms, or if it will raise policy issues.

It is worth repeating—most of what some people call "lobbying" on Capitol Hill simply means requests for casework assistance. Soldiers wanting compassionate leave; people who have lost immigration papers; the devout who object to the fact that Civil Service exams are scheduled on religious holidays; brigadier-generals wanting promotions; government employees who think that they have not been treated fairly from a personnel standpoint (a staff member of the Senate Armed Services told me a dozen years ago that, as of that time, most of the personal visits made to the staff of the committee dealt with personnel matters in which officers were interested! This may not have been literally true, of course, but it suggests a considerable volume of such visits); taxpayers who claim unfair treatment by the Internal Revenue Service; students wanting help in writing a term paper or a thesis;[6] old people and veterans concerned with their benefits and pensions; people who are in trouble because of some government action or other (land-taking for example)—all these and many more create the congressional workload! An example of what is normally casework being so handled as to raise a policy issue: A couple of years ago an Oregon congressman placed a young woman on his appointment list to the military academy!

If most petitioners visited congressional offices in person, it would be easier to distinguish them from true Washington lobbyists or representatives. They do not. But sometimes they are

---

[6] I do not know if this is still true, but in an agency where I worked, years ago, term papers and possibly master's theses were in fact being written at congressional request; these may have been mostly for congressmen, staff, and family, rather than for constituents, but there were at least some requests from constituents, passed on to us, and processed.

spoken for by attorneys or other professional people, who are indistinguishable from lobbyists in appearance, manner, and approach. And, often enough, Washington representatives, out of good nature or because they feel coerced, handle cases brought to them by some member of the trade association or of the university faculty, etc.

It is impossible to tell by looking at them that members of two of the most prominent groups of casework petitioners are not lobbyists or Washington representatives. These are:

a. Agents or officers of municipalities, counties, special districts, universities, school systems, hospitals, and other public or semi-public bodies. Congressmen ask assistance for such agencies in getting grants or contracts.

b. And, of course, business executives ask for congressional help in getting contracts or aids—or on the location of bases and projects. Here, senators and congressmen can make a very discernible difference; would the defense aerospace industry in Cambridge and on Route 128 have grown as much as it has if Massachusetts had not had Saltonstall, McCormack, and Martin? And if Connecticut had had men in Congress in any way comparable to these able "operators," would not there have been more defense work channelled to Connecticut?

Now, note that the great majority of pleas and requests do not normally involve anything that Congress is likely to do itself. The typical request for casework help does not demand anything that the individual congressman can do much about directly; generally, his only practical response to a petition is to intercede with a bureau. There are exceptions to this general statement, but they are complex and, not in terms of the general point, central. Of course, to any particular petitioner, they can make all the difference in the world.[7]

---

[7] The first exception is provided by private bills, designed to take care of particular cases. These may either be exceptions to general law or they may provide for cases not really covered by general law. A typical case is a

II.

Some senators and congressmen—for instance, Senator McCarran of Nevada, Chairman of Judiciary for some years—acquire great power over a department. It was often said that Senator McCarran had more power over the Immigration and Naturalization Service of the Department of Justice than any Attorney-General. To the extent that this was true, one reason was that he had utilized the opportunity for special treatment and special favors, arising from his committee post. In securing or prohibiting specific exemptions from general immigration acts, the constant flow of requests made him a man whose goodwill was significant to many persons, including notably many of his fellow senators. For most of them had articulate constituents who wanted a

---

measure providing that specified individuals may enter or remain in the United States, *despite* quota and other prohibitions under general immigration law. The second exception is what may be called semi-private bills, those which ostensibly are somewhat general, but in fact apply to a limited group of persons in a particular way. For instance, when some of the Portuguese islands were ravaged by volcanic action, a bill permitting the non-quota entry of a certain group of island residents to the number of around 5,000 was passed.

The third, and probably most important exception, is that the Appropriations Committees do, frequently, pass on specific measures of specific interest to specific businesses, towns, etc. In the House, however, excepting the Chairman and ranking opposition member, members have direct influence only on a specific panel. The late Chairman, John Taber, tried to place Republicans on panels (subcommittees) where they could not help their districts. Fourth: other committees, notably Armed Services (described to me by one of its officials as "basically a real estate committee") and Public Works, do authorize or refuse to authorize projects and installations. And Ways and Means can provide specific helps. Still, at least two-thirds of the members of the House serve on committees where there is little they normally can do about specifics of the sort for which people petition.

Seventy years ago, favors of the sort just listed—and others which the Congress had the power then to confer, but has since delegated, such as setting specific tariffs—may well have constituted the bulk of special interest favors available from the Federal government. But as the Federal government has grown, the number of favors which it can confer have tremendously increased; and most favors are now *directly* conferred by the executive branch.

chance to get a relative or friend or technically skilled employee into the United States, despite quota restrictions.

Yet, it took an unusual kind of skill to master such power. Who can imagine Wiley of Wisconsin, or Langer of North Dakota, ranking Republicans on Judiciary during McCarran's Chairmanship, exerting a tenth of the power as Chairman that McCarran held?

Another example of a man who did much for his constituents, chiefly because of his position, was John Taber, for many years ranking Republican, and for two sessions, Chairman of House Appropriations. In preparing an article about him,[8] I talked with a number of his constituents. One of them, an attorney and a Liberal Democrat in the tradition of Mrs. Roosevelt and Governor Lehman, said to me in 1948, "I despise most of what that man stands for. But I have to support his reelection. It would take me three weeks a year more in Washington if he weren't there; he does so much for me." Considering the nature of the attorney's clients, I suppose these services concerned taxes, accounting on wartime arrangements, hang-overs from price control, information on labor issues, etc.

Friendship with such congressional operators can be worth a great deal to a Washington representative or favor-seeker; the trouble is that it takes years for most men to build up such powerful operations, and, having acquired it, they are not accessible to all and sundry.

III.

In understanding how congressmen react to Washington representatives and lobbyists, the favor-seeking patterns just described are crucially important. For, *most congressmen*—and, even more,

---

[8] Published as "John Taber—Watchdog of the Treasury," in *Zion's Herald* (August 1, 1948), a polemic, not an analytic, article of a sort I would not now be likely to write.

their staffs (for casework is often delegated to assistants)—*are in the business of trying to get favors for people, or, and this is as important, of going through the motions of trying to get favors for people.* Most of the time, their efforts at getting favors, or of appearing to try to get them, involve requests, appeals, demands, the passing-on of information, to some agency or bureau in the executive branch. Sometimes, these efforts at favors involve requests or pleas to other members of the Congress serving on committees which can handle the request (it is rare to *demand* something from fellow congressmen). Not infrequently, efforts at getting favors involve dealings with other levels of government or private organizations. Some senators and congressmen do casework with state or city or even foreign governments or refer cases to private social welfare agencies, veterans' organizations, and the like.

Occasionally the senator or congressman merely has to try to persuade fellow members of his own committee. But it is only on very rare occasions that he has the capacity to confer the favor by his own decision.

The natural tendency of congressmen and senators to do favors (or appear to be doing them) is reenforced by the fact that many of them have a background in state or local politics, or in the politics of, for instance, veterans' or fraternal organizations. Favor-giving is, generally speaking, even more critical to a sense of political competence in these organizations than it is in national politics. Consequently, *any* request to many Capitol Hill offices is likely to be handled as an opportunity to confer a favor. Naturally, each congressman has a definite notion as to what kinds of favors may appropriately be asked of him. For instance, some congressmen are extremely reluctant to do favors for anybody outside their constituency. An extreme example of this: I was trying in 1953–1954 to interview selected members of the Ways and Means Committee, in connection with the study which led to *American Business and Public Policy*. Congressman

X's brother told my assistant very emphatically, "If Mr. Dexter is working for Massachusetts Institute of Technology, there are plenty of Massachusetts Congressmen for him to see. He is their business." So, I had a dozen friends of mine in his district write to the congressman, and then I received a personal call from him, early one morning, almost begging me "to come down and see me, anytime, anytime at all."

Some congressmen are ready, willing, and eager to do what they regard as "casework favors," so that they can be free to do what they want on serious, legislative issues. But, again, what is serious to one man, is a constituency favor, so far as another is concerned. Senator Fulbright, for instance, for obvious enough reasons, has strongly opposed the tendency of exchange scholars to stay in this country and to seek private immigration bills to permit them to do so if necessary; in his view, such exemptions destroy the purposes of the exchange program; they are to him policy issues. Yet, unquestionably, most of his colleagues who introduce such bills regard them as merely favors to the man in question, and even more to the university or research institute or business firm or friend who requests that it be done.

On the other hand, Senator Fulbright's record would suggest that he may regard certain actions as simply favors to the cotton growers, utilities, and textile interests in Arkansas. Whereas some senators regard these very same matters as involving profound issues of far-reaching legislative importance, which they never handle as favors.

The favor-trading, favor-giving orientation of Congress is well illustrated by the following: I asked the knowledgeable assistant to the senator from a certain state why Congressman X in that state had voted against the Speaker and the leadership and the interests of his district and the committee and his own committee on several votes involving foreign trade. "Well, you see, Jack Q is a pal of Jim Y (congressman from an adjoining district but of quite different economic character); they usually travel home together and everything; and Jack knew that Jim absolutely *had* to vote against the leadership on these matters; all those rubber-workers and textile-makers in his home district are yelling like hell about Japanese imports. And Jim did not like to be left alone, out there, naked, for everybody to see, voting against the Speaker and the committee report and everything. So, Jack voted with Jim to make Jim look better." And, of course, some day, if other issues of more importance to Jack develop, he can count on Jim's voting alongside him, regardless of anybody.

In dealing with most congressmen, most Washington representatives will be well-advised to present their position, where possible, as a request for a favor, in the form in which that congressman and his staff like requests to be made, backed up by the kind of support which that congressman appreciates. I suspect one reason for the unpopularity of some serious-minded lobbyists who stress the public interest is that they do not ask for favors; they come to *tell* congressmen what the latter *ought* to be thinking. Many congressmen, that is, do not concede that anybody else knows more than they do about the public interest; but they are willing and eager to do favors.

On almost any matter, if the congressman is going to get anywhere with it, he is going to have to ask a favor from someone else. This means he may have to expend some of his capital, his stock in trade, his ability to be listened to.

So, the best thing of all for a Washington representative is to be able to approach a congressman or senator with something that will somehow enable the latter to increase his political capital—to increase his prestige, his publicity value, his ability to get campaign contributions or speaking dates, his respect from his colleagues, his influence downtown in the bureaus or back home. As a practical matter, some approaches to congressmen by Washington representatives do involve a net credit potential in prestige and power. For instance, when Dorothy Detzer of the Women's International League for Peace and Freedom and her associates, persuaded Senator Gerald Nye of North Dakota to sponsor the inquiry which became the investigation of the "merchants of death," he became (to be sure, reportedly, contrary to his own expectations) as an outcome, one of the best-known members of the Senate, more in demand on college campuses than any other Republican at that time. Or it is widely believed that the tie-in between the late Senator Bridges of New Hampshire and the so-called "(Free) China lobby" was beneficial to the former in several ways. And, whoever (perhaps the National Association of Retired Persons) persuaded Senator Winston Prouty of Vermont to sponsor, and carry against administration and committee objections, the payment of $35 a month to older people not receiving other government checks, did not hurt Senator Prouty; the latter was not at the time as well known as many of his colleagues, but this amendment spread his name among some people inside and outside of Vermont.

But congressmen are like most people nowadays, they have learned to be cautious. Too many of the people who come in and see them (*even quite experienced people*) try to sell them on something which will not basically help the congressman's career or reelection. So, like housewives dealing with a door-to-door salesman, or publishers listening to an author with a book which "will make a million dollars," they are skeptical. An idea should, if possible, be presented in such a way that it obviously helps the congressman; but the congressman should be led to sell himself on its advantages to him.

IV.

One story illustrates the nature of favors, the advantages of having a skilled Washington representative, the tendency of members of Congress just to go through the motions, and a typical relationship between congressmen and the executive branch. I was questioning an industrialist in a medium-sized city,[9] who (a) since there was no trade association in his rather small industry, and, since he was, unlike his competitors, independently wealthy, acted from time to time as the industry's "action agent" in Washington, and (b) was really as much or more interested in the missionary activities of his denomination as in his industry.

He explained that the industry was harassed by competition from foreign-made goods. So, he went to his senator, whom he had known all his life, and to whose campaigns, I suspect, he had always contributed. He explained the issue to the senator and the latter's personal secretary, whom he had also known most of his life. He had a file of correspondence about the matter, which amounted to the senator having raised it with, as I now recollect, the State Department and the Tariff Commission. The latter agencies sent gobbledygookish replies, referring to statutes and regulations by number, which seemingly amounted to a statement: "We will look into the matter; we cannot be too encouraging." At that time, it was the obvious general policy of State (and probably of the Tariff Commission) to procrastinate about demands for action to restrict imports.

Later, the interview with the industrialist went on to his missionary interests. He told me in rather vivid detail how the government of India was making it difficult for the denomination's missionaries to bring in and use trucks, moving picture equipment, and school supplies. Naively, I asked: "And did you talk to the senator and his secretary about that, too?" Immediately and firmly, he replied: "No, what the dickens business is that of the senator's! That is the responsibility of Tom so-and-so in such-and-such a section of" either State or the organization for foreign aid, a section of which I personally never heard before or since. He told me all about it.

[9] Called New Zanzuel in Bauer, Pool, and Dexter, *American Business and Public Policy*, pp. 310–311.

Now, he was quite right that negotiations with the Indian government on this issue was the responsibility of this particular section (perhaps, also, of other branches of the executive, but not of the Congress). He was absolutely right that, constitutionally speaking, it was none of his senator's business. And, too, practically speaking, his senator would not have been a good source of referral and guidance on the matter.

But these things were also true of the foreign import issue with which he was concerned. Action on this matter was not, due to numerous laws passed in the preceding twenty years, any longer the direct responsibility of Congress. Help would have to come first from the executive branches.

The senator's office, of course, recognized this fact by referring the matter to the Department of State and the Tariff Commission. This is, typically, what senators and congressmen do with most requests for favors. They refer them to some branch of the executive. Very often, all they ask for is information—how should this thing be handled? What procedures should the aggrieved person follow?

But, note, that in this instance two things did not happen: a. the issue was not sharply explained by the senator's office to the administrative agencies—all the letters from the senator really said were "here is a problem," and b. the issue was not presented to all the administrative agencies which might have been able to take helpful action.

There are, for instance, provisions administered by the Treasury to make difficult certain kinds of selling below cost, "dumping." There are "Buy American" provisions which might apply to some branches of Defense and Interior which probably bought the product in question. There was nothing in the correspondence —or in my subsequent conversation with the senator's staff—to indicate that anyone there had thought that either of these routes might be helpful. It was clear that the senator's office was not prepared for the work of turning the complaint into a form with which the bureaucrats could grapple, and it was even clearer that the bureaucrats who replied to the senator's letters had no interest in figuring out how the issue could best be handled from the standpoint of the industry.

Now, there is no necessary reason why any senatorial or congressional staff assistant should be competent at such specification of issues. In general, in many instances, they get along about as well—and with considerably less bother—if they only "go through the motions." This particular senator was distinguished for a different kind of case service; he would, for instance, personally buy fashionable clothes in Washington stores for people who lived in rural parts of his constituency.

There are senatorial and congressional offices where my manufacturer interviewee would have got better referral than he did in this particular instance; or had the constituent known what precisely to ask for, this senator would have been more helpful.

But the case basically illustrates the importance of having a Washington representative. To be sure, so far as the particular matter of foreign imports is concerned, it may have been more of a nuisance, at the time, than a crisis, to the industry. But there were, the manufacturer said, other problems—problems, of course, on tax policy, and problems with scarce materials (this was just after the Korean War), and problems on labor, which both he and others in the industry faced. Apparently, he handled them as the industry's substitute for a trade association in much the same way; they had been sent through the office of Senator Personal Service. It must have been chance if helpful handling was given any of them.

CONTRAST WITH WASHINGTON REPRESENTATION.

A skillful Washington representative would have found out, in the case of taxes or foreign imports or labor or scarce materials, what the issues were, and which should have priority. The senator's office, after all, had no way of knowing whether any of these issues were particularly critical (materials, actually, probably had been really most critical). *It would, ordinarily, be impolite for a congressional office to ask the kind of searching questions which a good Washington representative might ask.* And, too, a senator is unlikely to be in a situation where he would look foolish, if he did not know a good deal about the case. The Washington representative, to protect himself, has to find out the facts. For, only by finding out the facts, will he be prepared to defend his case, if he has to do so.

And a Washington representative, worthy of that name, would have formulated and reformulated the problem, so that it would fit into the right bureaucratic categories. Could it be a matter of anti-dumping? Is there some obscure provision of the Reciprocal Trade Act which would permit defensive action, and, if so, what facts are needed? Would any kind of "escape clause" action be feasible? Would there be any way in which the Buy American Act could be invoked? The plant was, as it happens, unionized; the president of the company, and his immediate assistants, knew nothing whatever about the international union, but just assumed it would be hostile—their experiences with unions were not unusually encouraging. But, in fact, in the particular case, there was a good chance that the international union would have cooperated with the industry. Would its help have been useful? Even if it would not have actually helped, nevertheless, on some aspects of the matter, such as those to be suggested in the next paragraph, its advice would have been valuable; and that advice could have been obtained just as easily as the senator's. In fact, the international union probably would have welcomed a chance to build a bridge to such employers as this one.

A really skillful Washington representative—one who saw his job in fullest perspective, as affecting policy outcomes, *however* they can be affected—would have seen, I believe, in the particular situation, a promising way out. Most consumers of this product (an extremely durable, expensive good) were, as it happened, professional groups. It also happened that, on the face of the facts as reported to me by the manufacturer, it would seem that the conditions of labor in the plants which were producing the foreign competing goods were such as to horrify most United States purchasers. A public relations campaign could have been organized, without any great expense, directed to the responsible officers of purchasing organizations. In the then dominant state of opinion in these organizations, such a campaign—reenforced presumably by salesmen for the U.S. industry—would have, almost certainly, led many buyers to be willing to pay somewhat more for the United States-made product. As further *illustrations* of the kind of technical issues which a competent Washington representative would have looked into: *and which most congressmen have not time to do:*

a. It is possible—though I do not think so—that there are some provisions in some labor standards legislation or international agreements for protesting importation of products, manufactured under the circumstances which these apparently were, into the United States. If there are any such provisions, it is probable that it would be extremely difficult or impossible to "prove" the facts as alleged by the American manufacturers. Such a possibility should not however be dismissed out of hand, partly because if any such provision exists, the effort to get it invoked might serve as a background for the publicity campaign just discussed—even though it could not really be invoked.

b. According to the manufacturer, one of their special problems arose in importing into Canada (which they, in common with most U.S. manufacturers, regard as within their domestic market). If it were established that the actual or potential Canadian market was significant enough to the industry to matter, there were three possible lines of approach:

1. to try to persuade the appropriate authorities in the State

Department to take up the matter of liberalizing the effective Canadian import requirements.

2. to find out if the U.S. industry had or could have any influence of its own in Ottawa, through which an Ottawa representative could work with the Washington representative.

3. to determine whether a public relations campaign on the labor standards issue, mentioned above, would for any reason backfire in Canada. My impression would be that it would have worked equally well there.

V.

This story is, of course, given for the sake of illustration. One of the most vital points it illustrates is this: *a Washington representative's obligation is that he find out what the problems really are and that he check on the facts.* Obviously, it would be impossible and most impolitic for a senator or congressman to try to make any such attempt. Often, a senator or congressman may suspect that the petitioner, the person who brings in a complaint, has not formulated the issue or the priorities and does not really know relevant facts. But, in the case just presented, how could Senator Personal Service's staff find out the salience of the issue about the Canadian market? This came up late in my conversation with the manufacturer; and he had never thought of presenting it to anyone. Yet, according to him and his assistants— once they thought of mentioning it—it was vital. And, if they had raised it with the Senator, could the Senator have been expected to check out vague estimates of a potential Canadian market of 10 to 15 percent of total output? Or could the Senator have been expected to weigh the relative importance to the industry of materials allocation, foreign imports, labor issues, tax matters? Suspecting that priorities had not been thought through and investigated, it makes perfectly good sense that the Senator *only* "went through the motions," and that the bureaucrats sent back obfuscating answers to the Senator's inquiries. At most, then, what the manufacturer, his attorney (a local man, not a Washington lawyer), and his assistants got out of the effort was a feeling that somebody had paid some attention to them and that they had fulfilled their obligation to the rest of the industry.

There is a familiar saying that "a man who has himself for a client has a fool for a lawyer." Like all folk generalizations, this is occasionally untrue; but it is true, where the man in question does not know in detail the professional and legal issues involved, and where the issue is important. So, also, with Washington representation. An unsophisticated, untrained man—manufacturer, county official, or whatever he may be—should either acquire expertise about government relations, or he should hire somebody who has it, if his relationships with the government are important to his organization. He cannot rely on Congress!

The characteristic point in this case was that the manufacturer suspected that government policy in at least four matters was actually or potentially of great moment to his firm, and to the entire industry, for which he was acting. But he did not know. I suspect that careful study would perhaps have shown that foreign imports were not a problem of moment, and that the effort I have suggested would not be worthwhile; but, before approaching the Senator, it would have been helpful to find how much effort it was worth! I suspect that tax policy and materials allocation regulations were of considerable importance, in ways which the manufacturer did not understand as well as in ways which he did. I suspect that a skillful Washington representative could have found helpful, unexpected allies (for instance, in the particular case, among church and professional organizations) on the materials allocation matter. But, again, this should have been checked out. If it turned out that these two issues mattered, and the other two, relatively, did not, a sophisticated client would have cooperated with the Washington representative in asking the Senator's help in specific ways on the two which mattered

—and not wasted the Senator's time on the other two, foreign imports and labor.

The ironic twist to the situation is that, at least in large measure, the manufacturer in his other role as chairman of a denominational missionary committee, had become fairly sophisticated about Washington representation. He knew who, actually, could take the relevant action and how to approach him. In this regard, he had been briefed and educated by his predecessor as chairman, and by the full-time paid staff of the denomination and possibly of the National Council of Churches. But there had been no such briefing, no such education, in his business capacity, so he handled that whole relationship amateurishly and ineffectively. Who says business is necessarily more politically sophisticated than "naive" churchmen?

VI.

Put in general terms, the point of the story is: *referral to obvious sources can and will be made by a congressman or senator. Guidance in using the full range of government resources is more than most senators or congressmen give, or can be expected to give. Such guidance has to come from elsewhere. Hence, Washington representation.* What use then are senators or congressmen? Basically, senators and congressmen can often:

a. Get information more quickly and fully than the constituent or the representative. Government agencies are generally supposed to attach priority to congressional requests, and many of them do so. Many of them will go to great trouble to answer a request from a congressman.

For instance, a congressional request to appropriate branches in Commerce, Labor, and State might have produced full documentation on the labor practices of the industry's major foreign competitor. It would have been important, however, to know which sections of the State, Commerce, and Labor Departments might be able *and willing* to find the relevant information. Some people in the State Department, including some who were at the time engaged in legislative liaison, would have interpreted the request as a threat to United States relations with the foreign country involved; others would have inquired willingly from international agencies as to pertinent information.

b. Congressional staffs can help check and add to the inquirer's notions as to agencies which should be asked for information or action; there are congressional offices which on a given topic are as good as a Washington representative (for instance, on anything relevant to the major manufacturing industries of New England, Senator Saltonstall's office would have been nearly as good as a competent Washington representative), and, of course, there is a lot of exchange between congressional offices. But, usually, once the inquirer has some idea of where to go and why, he can profitably discuss the matter with the staff of congressional offices, to see if they have something additional to suggest, or some experience which will help shape his questions.

c. Congressmen can provide access—often quickly—to most agencies or bureaus. Sometimes this can be a disadvantage; if the decision is actually going to be made at a section chief level, and a senator or congressman makes a big issue of the favor, the first interview may be with an under secretary, who does not know the facts and who simply wastes time. But more often it is an advantage.

d. Congressmen and their staffs can in a good many instances, but by no means all, add to the likelihood that a matter will be considered favorably by the department or section handling it.

Members of relevant committees, who have established a friendly relationship with the agencies with which they deal, or who seriously frighten these agencies, are perhaps most likely to influence a favorable response. If, in addition, the member has a staff assistant or supervises a committee clerk who thoroughly understands the procedures of the agencies in question, then he can be extremely influential in a few cases. Even so, there is little he can achieve in regard to most requests, simply because to do anything about them would involve altering a set of procedures or traditions, or run counter to the agencies' notion of what is permissible and safe. For instance, a shrewd bureaucrat will foresee that if one change is made, in the seemingly reasonable general direction requested by Member X, at the moment, then other organizations and interests will come in, perhaps sent over by Member X himself, a year or two hence, bitter about the effects of the change upon them, and insisting on a return to previous practice.

At the opposite extreme from the influential members just described is a member who has been in Congress for a few years, long enough to make an impression, who is serving on an unimportant and irrelevant committee, who has attracted attention in the bureaucracy because he sends over a number of people with impossible and improper requests, who is not at all specific about what he wants done for the petitioner, and who is in the habit of "throwing his weight around" even in circumstances where he has no leverage.

Most members, of course, fall somewhere between these two extremes. And a member who may be influential with one agency, say the Office of Economic Opportunity—simply because he is regarded as their sort of person—may have a negative impact in some old-line bureau in an established department. A skillful Washington representative will try to determine which congressional ally will be useful where; he would hardly expect, for instance, a request from Eugene McCarthy, at the present moment, to be especially well-regarded by some bureaus in the Department of Defense, whereas it might be attended to, favorably, in an agency staffed with intellectual "liberals." Most reputations are not as clear and easy to judge as his, of course, and take more specialized knowledge of how the member is regarded by whom.

  e. Sometimes, if he is sufficiently interested, or becomes so, a congressman can aid in a publicity campaign, which helps achieve the purposes of the client or employer—even though no direct governmental action is involved. Senator Personal Service was not, by temperament or affiliation, likely to be of help himself on the kind of publicity campaign suggested as worth considering in our story above. But his executive secretary was in close and continuing contact with prominent leaders of the party in the senator's state; at least one of these leaders might have been glad to lend himself to any such campaign. And, had the matter come up under the senator's successor, the latter might well have been delighted to participate in such an effort.

There is, of course, one other thing which often makes it useful to consult a member or his staff fairly early:

f. It may turn out, ultimately, that some kind of legislative action is called for. If the senator's office has been in touch with the development of the situation, it is more likely to take an interest and of its own volition suggest appropriate legislative action. But, against this, must be traded off the effort and bother involved in dealing with the congressional office, if it turns out not to be necessary, if otherwise, the whole matter could have been more easily handled directly with the relevant section of the executive, which is often the case. Intermediaries usually take time and often misinterpret situations—even congressional intermediaries.

6

THE WASHINGTON REPRESENTATIVE AND CLARIFICATION OF CLIENTS' PROBLEMS: "GUIDANCE"?

Several Washington representatives have summed up their contribution to their clients in such terms as "Information . . . guidance . . . influence." Granted at first hearing, "guidance" or the synonym used by some, "education," of the client sounds pretentious. Clients and employers, on the other hand, sound too commercial. They often tend to feel that they are buying a direct service, just as they would buy a commodity. They believe the Washington representative does for them just exactly what they, individually, could do for themselves if they had the time and the Washington contacts.

If people who sell their advice on government relations are merely selling a service—like the boy who comes around to shovel snow or cut hedges—then such an interpretation of Washington representation would be correct. But, in fact, Washington representation is a profession; the Washington representative is less like the boy who comes around to cut hedges than like the landscape architect who advises the home owner how hedges should fit into the total layout and ecology of a property.

I.

As preface to the following, let me repeat again: In practice it is not nearly this complicated; all this rarely takes place with one client except over a long period of time!

Many clients and employers do not like, naturally enough, the idea that people whom they have hired are guiding and educating them. Nevertheless, a good many clients *are* educated or guided along the following lines:

A. *The most important service of Washington representatives to clients and employers is teaching the latter to live with the government and in the society. That is, Washington representatives instruct a good many clients how to adapt, accommodate, and adjust.*

They do this in three ways:

1. by showing the client and employer that there are paths around, out, and through, if one is willing to settle for "half-a-loaf," and to settle for incremental gains or for avoiding substantial losses, even though one does not get what (one thinks) one is justly entitled to;

2. by convincing clients and employers that there has, indeed, been an all-out effort, that the government has handled the case fairly and that there is nothing further to be done; and

3. by interpreting for clients and employers in terms which

they can appreciate the positions of (a) the government and of (b) other interests which the government has to take into account.

It is the *interpretation* which is crucial; this can be done better by Washington representatives than by information programs from government, because the competent Washington representative can and does use the client's language[1]—which bureaucrats cannot do.

Such interpretation is feasible partly because the Washington representative himself has, or acquires, more sympathy with the government and with competing interests than the client. It happens, too, in the case of Washington representatives who are lawyers, because of the legal tradition that the client ought to be informed of the "case against him," and of the obstacles in trying to get his way.

It does not happen as frequently or as freely as might be hoped. Some Washington representatives simply tell employers or clients what the latter want to hear. And some clients are able

[1] There are inherent tendencies in any bureaucratic system which make its explanatory language seem hostile or dryly unsympathetic and uncomprehending to many of those affected by it. And, in any event, each interest, each point of view, has its own special vocabulary, which presents issues in the way most acceptable to it. This matter of vocabularies is discussed in relationship to similar problems in my "Role Relationships and Conceptions of Neutrality in Interviewing," *American Journal of Sociology*, 62 (1956). The general, systematic background for this kind of awareness is best stated by Kenneth Burke in "Attitudes Towards History," *New Republic*, 1937.

See also L. A. Dexter, "Check and Balance Today" in A. de Grazia, ed. *Congress The First Branch*, (New York: Doubleday and Company [Anchor], 1967) to be reprinted in revised form in my forthcoming book on Congress (Chicago: Rand McNally and Company, 1969–1970).

I have spoken of "competent" Washington representatives in the text. One of the real temptations to the inexperienced Washington representative and one of the real dangers for the man who comes direct from the bureaucracy to Washington representation is that he may either out of pretentiousness or sheer habit use the specialized Washington vocabulary in a way which puzzles or confuses his clients. The need is, of course, to interpret in whatever terms are familiar to them, not to repeat the bureaucratic lingo.

to close their minds to anything of a disturbing nature. And there is not, unfortunately as yet, any general awareness either by clients or by Washington representatives that interpretation is their function. A partial (and incomplete) parallel: Many object to government tax laws and policies. But a good tax attorney does not show how to evade taxation or how to fight tax laws to the death; instead he shows people how to live with and adjust to them, at minimum cost and strain.[2]

B. A second significant aspect of guidance arises out of the fact that most organizations have many opportunities and problems with the government. *A Washington representative can help his clients balance sets of opportunities and sets of problems against each other and determine priorities between them.* He can do this by:

1. judging which problems have the best hope of being worked out favorably to the organization, at the least cost in total resources;

2. finding out what facts are necessary to convince responsible government agencies of the merit of the organization's claims, or to obtain the cooperation of responsible outsiders;

3. in dealing with one and two he is likely to raise the question whether particular problems and opportunities when closely analyzed appear to have the same degree of importance as when reacted to impressionistically. Of course, the Washington representative in a well-managed organization is not by any means the chief person who does this; chief executives do it,

[2] Of course, I am not for a moment denying that there are cases where organizations have a point of view which must lead them into direct opposition to the government—Puerto Rican nationalists, supporters of Albizu-Campos, a few years ago would have been an example of this and nowadays an example would be the more intense opponents of the Vietnam War. That is to say, some organizations are not willing, for whatever reason, to accommodate, or are not able to do so. But this book is written for those organizations that are able to accommodate. Actually, it is probable that organizations with any range of interests will be able to accommodate on some matters, even if they directly challenge the system on others.

and in many organizations others also engage in "operations research."

C. Where there is a well-planned relationship between client and Washington representative, the latter is kept in touch with major aspects of what the organization is planning. Bearing its activities and prospects in mind, as he moves around Washington, *he may encounter opportunities for the organization.* It may turn out, for instance, that management research in the Department of Defense or population analyses in the Bureau of the Census could be helpful to the client.

D. It is almost never the case that a given problem or claim can be met through one and only one channel. There are nearly always alternative ways of solving the same problem, of obtaining the same sort of opportunity, in a society as complex, fragmented, and diversified as ours. *The Washington representative can suggest different ways of dealing with a problem; and he can evaluate their relative advantages and disadvantages.*

In making such assessment, he will bear in mind the probability that some good ways of handling a problem or of obtaining an opportunity may not be predominantly governmental at all. For instance, in the illustrative history given in the preceding chapter, it might have turned out after study that the best way of fighting the foreign import menace to the industry in question would have been a public relations campaign. This campaign would have emphasized the offensive circumstances under which the foreign product was manufactured in such a way as to discourage United States consumers from taking advantage of the slight saving on it. The only relevance the government would have had would have been as a source of information in such a case.

Or, it might well be that the most immediately productive way of getting certain firms to control their pollution of air and water would be through major stockholders—assuming, for instance, some of their major stockholders were non-profit organizations,[3] like universities or foundations or churches, or even that individual stockholders were conservationists.

E. Actually, any issue of government relations may involve guidance of the client by the Washington representative. For instance, take coalitions and alliances in Washington. The Washington representative should suggest to his client the possibility of establishing working relationships with other groups. For instance, in the illustrative case history in the preceding chapter, it was suggested that cooperation with the union in the industry might have been helpful to the industry in regard to issues of moment; and, for instance, the steel industry will be helped in its present demand for quotas on imported steel if it gets the priority cooperation of the United Steelworkers. But there are reasons, both in the industry of the case history and in steel, why some firms are hesitant or hostile as to joint action with the union. Yet, in fact, the union in each case has political "muscle" and Washington know-how which many firms do not have.

Another example of where a representative might have to guide his clients into cooperation with groups towards which there is not initially warm feeling: Persons representing "liberal" state governments or city administrations are likely during the next few years to push for Federal supports and aids for police in many ways. In some of their efforts, they could receive help from right-wing organizations which emphasize "Support Your Local Police." These right-wing organizations may be influential with some southern and western congressmen, whereas these same congressmen would react negatively to an appeal from representatives of big city mayors or urban governors.

A third vital field of useful guidance may be *campaign con-*

---

3 Indeed, in the whole area of ecology, it would seem that the most direct influence foundations and universities could have would be as stockholders; I have no knowledge that any foundation or university has ever tried to exercise its direct influence as a stockholder to prevent or remedy contamination of the atmosphere.

tributions. The Washington representative should especially guide the client here as to preserving access or rewarding specific help in the past in instances where the client is strenuously opposed to the general stand of the senator or congressman in question.

Before continuing this discussion, *it should be emphasized that there is no intention here of defending every feature of the United States political system as it exists.* But Washington representatives, like anyone else engaged in politics, must take account of the rewards, punishments, and reciprocation of favors which do currently govern behavior. A Washington representative, who holds the good-government notion that the campaign contribution system as it operates is undesirable, might propose changes in the system; but, as long as the system remains as it is, he must take it into account in his work with his clients.

The Washington representative should not, however, generally put himself in the position of having the final say-so on campaign contributions, and similar favors. But he should have the right to argue strenuously that when campaign contributions are considered, the client follow the general practice of similar groups having Washington interests and that the position *on other matters* of senators or congressmen be treated as distinctly secondary.

For instance, there certainly are cotton, textile, and utility interests in the South to whom Senator Fulbright's views on Santo Domingo and Vietnam are repulsive; but, to the extent that he has continued to help them on their specific needs, their Washington representatives should have insisted that if he lacked campaign funds in 1968, they should contribute. Vice versa, the reportedly hawkish position of Congressman Bolling of Missouri in 1966 may have been abhorrent to some strong civil rights and education groups in the country; but if he needed financial help in that year, they should have given it to him because of his services to them on their own concerns. Or—more extreme at the time—during the Truman administration, fur interests in the old Northwest had received help from Joseph McCarthy of Wisconsin, *Republican*, and, probably, had a better prospect of effective aid from Hubert Humphrey of Minnesota than from any other *Democratic* senator. Consequently, any Washington representative of that industry ought to have been able to insist that members of the industry contribute to McCarthy and to Humphrey regardless of any disapproval that individual furgrowers felt for either man's general policy impact, and, of course, regardless of the fact that, in general, the politics of the two men were sharply opposed.

Aside from campaign contributions, a Washington representative of a big interest ought to be able to suggest retainers, grants, employment, etc., for friends or potential friends in the legislative and executive branches—until such time as these practices are effectively forbidden. This includes of course jobs for family, campaign associates, and even potential rivals.[4]

II.

Other specific examples of some aspects of guidance are provided by the case history in the last chapter. If the manufacturer who asked help from Senator Personal Service had had a competent and imaginative Washington representative, the latter would have:

a. Found out what facts were needed to test the industry's belief that foreign imports constituted a serious threat, and particularly what facts would be likely to influence appropriate government agencies to take remedial action.

b. Tried to assess the relative severity of the different prob-

[4] In fact one of the most basic aids any congressman or senator can receive is an offer of employment to a potential primary opponent which the latter can not resist; and sometimes a particularly attractive potential candidate in the opposing party can be taken out of the race by similar means. Another great need in some instances is a job for a former associate, who has, for some reason, become an embarrassment or a threat, which will take him out of the district.

lems which the industry faced (foreign imports, taxes, labor policy, and tax regulations) and to determine where there was the best hope of success in getting action favorable to the industry.

Generally speaking, a good Washington representative would have given rough weights to these different issues, based upon a balancing of the severity of the problem as against the possibility of achieving successful remedial action.

c. In establishing such a rough assessment of priorities, he also would have taken into account the possibility of getting effective help from outside the manufacturing group—from the union or from other industries with similar problems, or from professional groups, or from officials of the towns and cities where the industry has plants, etc., etc.

And additionally, on the one hand, Senator Personal Service was no doubt glad to go through the motions of doing a favor for a prominent constituent who had contributed to his campaigns. But, on the other hand, the Senator's ties and affiliations, in general, clearly were with importing and exporting interests and with their general liberal trade line. Neither he nor his staff could be expected to go that extra mile to get protection for a small industry, unless it could be established that it really was faced with catastrophe or that failure to do so would hurt the Senator at the polls. These contingencies were not at all likely; nor was it likely that any other senator or congressman from the state in which the plant of the manufacturer with whom I talked was located would be sympathetic to protection.

Therefore, if it was decided, after calculation, that foreign imports really were a major threat, then a competent Washington representative would have undertaken another kind of guidance. The Washington representative would have established which members of Congress, from other states might be more helpful: (a) because plants of the industry were in their districts, and (b) they generally sympathized ideologically with protection, and/or (c) they resented the low wage and chauvinistic characteristics of the nation in which the foreign producer was located. Under the circumstances, the representative would have tried to persuade Mr. Industralist and other industry leaders that some of them (particularly those whose plants were in the appropriate areas geographically) should join in talking to these congressmen and senators.

7

INFLUENCE
INFORMATION
INTELLIGENCE

What Government Relations Can Not
and What It <u>Can</u> Provide

According to the Washington representatives quoted at the beginning of the last chapter, they can provide their clients with "guidance . . . information . . . influence." The phrasing is neat. But it is an oversimplification.

For, in fact, it is only on rare occasions that Washington representatives can really "provide," or "offer," that is to say, sell or rent influence. The notion, however, that this can frequently be done is common; it confuses clients, employers, potential clients, journalists, and a good many observers of government.

The best way to show the irrelevance of the notion to most Washington representation is to start out with a discussion of some typical occasions when influence is actually supposed to have been sold or rented. This provides a contrast with the more characteristic and realistic ways in which Washington representatives can help clients exert influence: *by discovering for the clients facts and techniques which permit the focusing and orienting of previously unexercised sources of influence.*

Reflections about the discovery of such facts and techniques lead directly into consideration of the kinds of information which a Washington representative can usefully provide his client or employer. In summary, the Washington representative must select, process, and handle information so that it becomes "intelligence," in the sense in which that word is used in military planning. For, in one way or another, clients and employers are concerned with actions or contemplated actions; and information is only useful to them if it affects plans for action.

I.

Influence can be most effectively sold or rented—from the client's standpoint, purchased—when the issue is that of awarding a specific favor. A contract is given to a corporation. A pardon is granted so-and-so. A tax decision benefits such-and-such a company. Broad issues of policy do not ordinarily arise on such matters. People who are, *chiefly*, concerned with them are not (in the sense in which the terms are used in this book) as such engaged in "Washington representation" or "government relations."

Nevertheless, of course, a good many Washington representatives spend part of their time on issues of policy and the rest on contracts, favors, special awards. Does it pay a client to try to hire somebody who has special influence, if part of the work in Washington is to get special favors?

Obviously, the answer to any such general question may vary with specific cases. But, ordinarily, it is of dubious value to the client.

First: There is rarely any way of telling whether influence or "pull" really did make the difference. The requirements of bureaucracy and the insistence upon honesty in government operate so that there is no clarity on the matter. Even if a decision is made on the basis of pull, the client cannot be sure at all that this is so—the decision-making official will not furnish any proof to that effect.

Second: We hear a good deal about ways in which special interests mislead public servants. There is also the reverse situation. Public servants may mislead—and do mislead—special interests in the following way.

They indicate to an organization that they will pay unusual attention to such-and-such a former employee or political supporter or relative. So, the organization hires the person. But, in fact, its claims are handled on their merits, just as they would have been anyway. With perhaps one additional handicap: some subordinates in the executive agencies, dealing with the organization are careful to lean over backward, because they foresee that if the political climate changes, some allegation of scandal may occur. So the organization, if anything, loses on the deal.

This is, as a matter of fact, one of the best ways in which politicians can provide for friends and allies and supporters.

There is a story told about Speaker Rayburn, and probably also about other distinguished politicians, which illustrates the point. Some time after he had become majority leader, a man came to him, who had done substantial favors for him years before in Texas. "What," said the Congressman, "can I do for you?"

"Just this—let me be seen with you! Let me walk with you from your office to the floor or over to dinner. That's all."

"That's all?" commented the Congressman. "You ask a lot less than most!"

"Yes," replied the man, "if I am seen enough with you, people will think I am somebody."

Probably, the somebodies who really counted in this story were interests engaged in hiring a Washington representative. And the man could have made a good thing, financially, out of the situation. Would his clients have got their money's worth? Only if the administrative agencies were as naive as they, and assumed because the man was seen in the Congressman's company in public, that he had real influence.

Yet, what less expensive way for the Congressman to repay past favors? And all things considered what great public disadvantage was involved?

Third: Influence is, in the nature of the case, usually a wasting asset. Mr. A may have helped Senator Y in a close election. Or Mr. C may have been prominent in the professional deliberations which took place before a new commissioner or bureau chief was chosen. And Mr. C may have played the decisive role in getting the professional group to support Commissioner X's candidacy.

It may be that Senator Y and Commissioner X are men who feel strongly that favors should be repaid, and would make a real effort to do so. Messrs. A or C might be able to get unusual favors from them—once or twice or possibly a third time. But then, two things would happen: first, the Senator and the Commissioner would feel that the account now balanced. And, second, due to the lapse of time, they would discount the favor; the Senator, for instance, would be more concerned about the next election than about a previous one.

On a one-shot basis, considerable favors can be obtained, no doubt, from some office-holders, because of gratitude or some other claim to special, personal attention. But a professional Washington representative will be extremely careful as to what claims he makes to be sure that he gets the best possible return on his earlier investment in the man's career, and, above all, he will be eager not to ask for too much. For a frequent source of ill will in politics (as in other human relations) is the demand by one man that he get better treatment than the other thinks he is entitled to.

We have supposed here that Senator Y and Commissioner X are men who acknowledge favors readily and gladly repay them. There are, of course, such men in politics. But there are others, like the late Mayor LaGuardia, who at the celebration, the evening of his first election, started his victory speech to his supporters: "I have one qualification for mayor. That is my capacity for monumental personal ingratitude."

More common, perhaps than either those who are grateful or who are purposefully ungrateful, are those who esteem the favor as demanding only limited gratitude; they have enough self-confidence, and they are personally sure they would have made it anyhow, so the man who helped them was after all investing in a sure thing.

Fourth: Also, almost anyone who has achieved a prominent position has *many* obligations, and ties, and considerations. A close associate of the late Governor Paul Devor of Massachusetts —one of those unfortunate men, temperamentally speaking, who did not forget obligations, who felt strongly he ought to try to repay them—said of the Governor:

"Poor Paul! He just could not get away from the people who had helped him over the years. He would walk out of the office and there in the waiting room would be half-a-dozen guys who had helped him in the great victory of 1948—who wanted something. And then on the other side of the office would be some fellows who had clung to him in the dreary, discouraging 1946 campaign for Lieutenant-Governor. And, if he went into the hall, he would probably see several fellows he had worked with in the Navy. Then, there would be a bunch who helped him in the 1940 Governorship race which looked like a close one. And, when he got downstairs there would be fellows who worked for him in the Attorney-General's office—where he did some pretty big things—and others who worked for him in the three A.G. fights—and don't forget that recount! that took a lot out of people. And, I am certain, when he got back home to Cambridge, there would be fellows who helped him in his campaigns for State Rep and others who started him out in politics. He could not shake them off!"

But the result was—and is—that no one man, no matter how much he may have done for a public figure, has as big a claim as he thinks he has—because there are a lot of others with big claims on the man.

II.

More or less the same sort of analysis might be made of other kinds of pull. A senator or a bureau chief may have a close personal friend, one who goes out of his way to entertain him and whose company he genuinely likes—and may do one or two or three favors for such a person. But in Washington, nowadays, after all, there are "as good fish in the sea as ever came out of it," and few important officials will risk serious jeopardy to their reputations by repeated acts of favor to some personal friend. Friends are easier to replace in Washington in 1968 than reputation and position.

It is, no doubt, possible to think of extreme and exceptional cases—blackmail or extraordinary sexual attraction—where the limitations here spoken of do not apply. But they are so exceptional as not to be important in any general discussion.

III.

I should also, perhaps, emphasize that I am speaking only of Washington in the period since 1933. I do not know enough about other capitals or about Washington before that date to say much about them. My suspicion is that in some state capitals, and in the capitals of some underdeveloped countries, pull is much more significant than in Washington today. It may have been more significant in Washington before the development of the present system of specialized communications. Nowadays, many people in a particular industry or profession throughout the country hear through all sorts of channels what is going on of interest to them in Washington. They well hear very quickly about, and some of them will resent, any allegations of favoritism. Before the development of newsletters, before the frequency of personal visits by professional and industry leaders to Washington, it may have been easy to get away with favoritism. It is more difficult now.

IV.

On this matter of "pull"—a clarification is in order. Influence is certainly desirable, and where one has influence or can easily acquire it, it is likely to be helpful. But the difference between "pull" and "influence" lies precisely in the notion that "pull" is illegitimate, influence legitimate. Trying hard to get pull is likely to have the difficulties referred to above and below. A Washington representative can very rarely—if ever—legitimize an organization or demand or movement which is not already regarded as legitimate. Of course, as we point out below, through the use of information and intelligence, a skillful Washington representative can channel or mobilize influence which would otherwise not be effectively employed.

V.

It is unquestionably easier to get specific favors through pull than to get general rules or regulations or policies established or changed through favor.

If a particular favor is worth enough to a given favor-seeker, it may be rational from his standpoint to exercise a good deal of pull in trying to get the favor. But it is rarely rational to exert a great deal of pull in order to get a general rule or regulation or policy established or changed; because one of two things is likely to be the case:

a. either competing interests are not very powerful or shrewd, so that the rule or regulation or policy could be established without pull; or

b. competing interests are powerful and shrewd enough so that if they discover that pull has been used, they will set to work to discover their own sources of pull. And, since public officials are under obligations to so many people, this can nearly always be done.

So, it is really not worthwhile—except under rather exceptional circumstances—to *try* to use pull to get a *general* policy established or changed. Opponents will offset such pull; the net result will merely be to increase the cost of doing business in Washington.

There are, apparently, state and city governments where middlemen exist who expect rake-offs on pull. But, in Washington, this is not the custom, and there is no advantage to most interests in acting so as to change that situation.

VI.

The preceding discussion does not mention one kind of influence which may be especially attractive to some clients or would-be clients. There are a number of persons who are advisors, money-raisers, confidants of political and administrative figures, and who themselves make a good deal of money out of being Washington representatives. Their relationship with the prominent is continuing. They will raise money in the next campaign as well as having done so in previous ones. They will be consulted on various difficulties. Their influence rests as much on future expectations as on past services.

But how much can and do they do for their clients?

This is one of the real mysteries of Washington. Certainly any client hiring them should know that normal notions about "conflict of interest" do not apply. They feel a greater loyalty to their political friends than to the clients who pay them. So, they will not push anything which would embarrass these political friends, even if such action would be helpful to the client.

Similarly—so far as their own time is concerned—if the political friends call on them, they will respond, often at the expense of effort which is committed to paying-clients. Consequently, in Presidential years, for instance, advisors of this sort are not particularly good representatives. They are too busy with other things.

Of course, some such people in fact only go through the motions themselves personally. They are the glamour boys of their firms; but they hire competent associates who do much the same sort of job any other Washington representative would do. The advantage for the firm may be that it can charge higher fees, because of the glamour boy's reputation. And, no doubt, the glamour boy does get quicker access, and more detailed information in some agencies—bureaucrats hope he will remember them the next time he talks to the President or to the Secretary of Defense. Whether this access outweighs the disadvantages of paying higher fees for what is not otherwise a different level of performance is a matter for the individual client to assess. Of course, many clients cheerfully pay for the privilege of hobnobbing with the famous and for the hope that they themselves will be introduced to the President or have a chance to breakfast with distinguished political leaders. If this is an expectation, it will often lead to disappointment; as a hope, how much is it worth?

There is one other disadvantage attaching to the employment of Washington representatives who are well known as advisors

to the famous. Those in Congress to whom they are *not* advisors
or potential advisors—usually the overwhelming majority—and
a good many bureaucrats are suspicious of them. So, although, on
the one hand, they may have more "influence" in some places
because of their close associations, they may have less in others
for the same reason. Anyone eager to do a neat study of balances
of influence might well try to calculate the balance in regard
to several such figures.

VII.

However, there are two kinds of influence which some Washington representatives can to an extent rent out. A man who is
respected for his integrity and judgment in a given field or by
a given senator can confer credibility, to a degree, upon a few
clients. If he takes a client, it will be assumed that the latter is
respectable—if nothing or little was known about the client before, or if the previous feeling was mixed. But, obviously, a man
who has earned this sort of respect has to be careful to keep it by
taking only respectable clients! He cannot practice according to
the lawyer's notion: "Everybody is entitled to a defense." Or, if
he does take a client whose case is weak, he has to be perfectly
open about it with his Washington associates. This sometimes
happens: a respectable Washington representative will say:
"Look, this client wants this. (For example, this foreign government). There's a lot of exaggeration and a lot of shoddiness in
the situation; but on the whole, this part of what they want
seems to me, after looking at it, justifiable, despite and disregard-
ing all these weaknesses. Will you look at it from that point of
view?" But, obviously, not very many Washington representatives can do this often; and it probably is a rare approach.

The other kind of what looks like "influence" that a good
many competent Washington representatives can sell is "access,"
the opportunity to be heard. Many clients present their own

cases too badly or too emotionally to be heeded. And, in any case, a man who has been around Washington for awhile has established contacts with people so that they will listen to him. But, although access is useful, *access is by no means the same as influence. It is simply a route towards influence—and in many cases, the route is blocked.*

A senior committee clerk or a committee chairman, a bureau chief or a White House aide, a commissioner in a regulatory agency, may listen a little sooner and a little longer to someone whom they already know. There are times when this can make the margin of difference. It probably is particularly important when the issue is new and the Washington representative has the rhetorical skill to define the issues in a memorable way, favorable to his client. (But, of course, many people who have access enough do not possess this skill).

But, in fact, a well-put case on any issue of importance will usually be heard by committee chairmen, White House aides, and commissioners anyway—regardless of who puts it. The occasions when access really "helps" *in the short run* are usually precisely those occasions when *in the long run* the case is doomed to failure. A person who has access, who is a friend or former co-worker, who is respected or politically prominent, can and will get a rehearing for an issue already decided; he can get consideration given to an extremely weak case, but he cannot get a favorable verdict. Access, that is, can drag out and delay a decision—which may at times be important—but it rarely influences the final verdict unless during the period of delay some change happens in the factual situation.

VIII.

Now we come to a restatement of a central emphasis of the entire book. *The kind of influence which a Washington representative can best provide is that arising from professional competence.*

A way of showing what this sort of professional competence consists in is by stressing why it is that most presentations to congressmen or bureaucrats—requests for changes in law or policy—coming spontaneously from those desiring the changes are not effective. They are ineffective because most people, making such presentations, do not take account of the history and complexity of the issue nor do they pay attention to the organizationally derived point of view of members of Congress or of the bureaucracy.

That is to say, issues—with the rarest exceptions—do not come before Congress or a bureau with a clean slate. On the contrary, in one form or another, executives, bureaucrats, legislative aides, and congressmen have dealt with closely related matters before. They know (or think they know) that any action to accomplish the particular purpose which interest A desires will be criticized by interests B, C, and D. They believe, on the basis of experience which is (or is thought to be) relevant, that if they actually do what an organization in terms of official policy presses for, sooner or later it may happen that some in that very organization protest the results of the change. As a parallel, it is well known that "good government" organizations at the local level which succeed in persuading or coercing public officials to enforce ordinances or taxing provisions "without fear or favor" sometimes discover that some of their own most prominent members protest the new dispensation quite vigorously. Similar problems happen in regard to numerous Federal decisions, although reasons of space forbid my citing those that come most quickly to mind.

An example wherein granting a request might create dissatisfaction somewhere else is provided by the case already discussed several times in this book. Suppose Senator Personal Service had taken the stand desired by the industry in his state; and some measure of action against foreign imports had been undertaken in consequence. In that same state there is a big port city, which probably has as high a proportion of business leaders opposed in principle to import restriction as any city in the country. They might conceivably have protested the action the Senator's other constituents desired. Or suppose that one of the biggest industries in the very town from which the protest came found, as is possible, that such an action made it more difficult to sell its products in the country which would be most hurt by the requested import restriction—perhaps the Senator a couple of years later would be trying some action to take care of a protest arising out of this situation.

Such aspects of the situation could have created problems for the Senator. Yet, to explain them briefly to Mr. Industrialist would have been dangerous; many people react to such an explanation by labelling the explainer as a "mere opportunistic politician." And to explain them at length would have taken more time than it would have been reasonable to expect from a senatorial office on what was after all a relatively minor issue from the Senator's standpoint.

But a competent Washington representative would have been aware of these aspects of the matter and of others like them.

A qualified Washington representative would be able to look at the situation, not only from the standpoint of the client, but from the standpoint of the Senator and his colleagues. With such an approach, he would be able to try to think of ways of asking for action which would lessen the risks to the Senator or he would have prepared himself to convince the Senator's staff that the threat of bother to the Senator was not really very great.

Similarly, since after all the real decisions would be made by administrative agencies, the Washington representative would be able to present the case to the latter in a way which minimized the risk of trouble to them, if it could be minimized, or, if it could not be, showed awareness of agency problems. From the standpoint of the agencies which might have done something to protect the industry, the significant question would almost certainly be: Why treat this industry differently? For, clearly, other industries might claim whatever protection was given this industry.

In fact, it is unlikely that a strong case could have been made for protection for the industry, in terms of the then prevailing viewpoints in Congress and the executive branch. But it is probable—if the industry's statements about barriers against selling its product in Canada were true—that on that matter there was a basis for special aid to the industry which would have been admitted both in Congress and in the State Department. And, so, the *"influence"* of the Washington representative would have consisted in his finding out to whom in government an acceptable and helpful case could be presented.

Likewise, if the industry could have accomplished something for itself in regard to materials allocation at the end of the Korean War, the "influence" of the Washington representative would have lain, precisely, in his ability to determine where and how presentations on this matter could best be made.

Now, a competent Washington representative is not, of course, concerned only with the arguments for or against a case, logically interpreted. He will recognize that in any governmental organization there are traditional ways of doing things, traditional hostilities, etc., which determine what is regarded as natural and proper. He knows that in any agency an issue is assessed partly in terms of that agency's own position in relationship to other agencies and the public, and partly in terms of the notions of propriety common in the agency. And he will be able to judge, in consequence, what agencies are the most likely to respond favorably to particular demands of a client at a given time. So, he will try to see what basis exists for presenting the case to the most favorably disposed agencies. And, vice versa, of course, if agencies to whom the case might most logically be presented are likely to be unsympathetic, he will inquire vigorously into alternative possibilities.

IX.

This kind of "influence" is secured by information about the internal workings of government. But a capable Washington representative should often spend effort in focusing *outside* influence upon governmental officials. For this purpose, he needs to know who outside government will actually have influence with those inside it who may pass on his case. He also needs to know how influential outsiders can be encouraged or persuaded to support it.

The most familiar example here is the Washington representative who stage-manages a presentation, brings in well-known experts to testify, and then gets constituents to see individual congressmen. The congressmen want to feel that important people favor the proposed bill; and they want also to feel that people in their own constituencies are paying attention to the matter and will appreciate what they do about it. Yet, in most cases, the experts would not have testified and the constituents would not have pushed the matter, unless the Washington representative had done the planning and coordinating.

Such presentations are often arranged by coalitions of groups and interests—the civil rights coalition consisted of well over 100 different organizations in 1964–1965. And, of course, a great deal of the exchange of information between representatives of different groups in such a case as this is about how to influence whom. One organization will feel it has a lead to a given congressman because of a religious tie; another will report that its representative talked with another congressman's executive assistant who seemed to be worried about a peripheral aspect of the proposal; a third will recollect that its national officers happen to be active in state politics in the home state of still another congressman and might be willing to call on him the next time he goes home. And someone else will suggest that, in fact, the newspaper coverage in certain states and cities from which key congressmen come has been poor—can anything be done about that?

Such coalitions exist on issues much more limited than civil rights. The lumber-paper company representatives in Washington meet together; the pharmaceutical company representatives also in practice meet together, in regard to such issues as the cost of Medicare items and how to handle drug regulations. In such coalitions there is a tendency to divide up responsibility, so that the representative of the company which has the most influence with a given committee chairman or the representative of the company which is the most involved in a specific issue becomes the "action agent" for that issue. He keeps the other representatives alerted; and then, on the next issue, some other company representative will become "action agent."

Coalitions have been developed more systematically in regard to legislation than in regard to relationships with administrative agencies. But this represents, more than anything else, the fact that all political reactions are a little behind the times. There probably have been coalitions, which I have not encountered, designed to influence some administrative agency. If there have not yet been full-fledged administratively oriented coalitions, there surely will be. Geography would count for less in coalitions of this sort, and professional alignment for more. A group, trying to influence the Public Health Service or the National Institutes of Health on some matter, might well divide officials up according to professional background—so that some members of the coalition would attempt to influence hospital administrators; others, surgeons; others, psychiatrists; and still others, professional civil servants.

Or consider an effort to get support for an Institute of Inter-American Studies, affiliated with the University of Puerto Rico, similar to the East-West Institute in Hawaii. Although congressional support would be useful and welcome in nurturing the idea, congressmen would not be of preeminent importance in the early period of its development. A member of the House Foreign Affairs Committee could, for instance, exert less influence than a section chief in A.I.D. in the early stages, unless he made it a real priority issue.

The advocates of such an institute would have to try to get support both inside and outside the government—from people with some weight in the educational-philanthropic community or in the field of Latin-American affairs.

The advocates of any proposal of this sort have to make at least nine separate kinds of calculations:

1. First, they have to determine who could kill the proposal by open hostility—in the particular case, the Governor of Puerto Rico almost certainly could, and the congressional delegate from Puerto Rico probably could. It is possible that real objection by various Pan-American or Inter-American secretariats would be lethal, also. And, at the University of Puerto Rico, substantial opposition from leading faculty members might well take place and could hurt a good deal.

It would not be necessary to secure the support of all or any of the above (though it would be helpful), but it would be wasteful to go ahead if they were seriously opposed.

2. What agencies in the Latin-American or Caribbean affairs field or in the educational-philanthropic community (or locally in Puerto Rico) might be in a position to provide necessary financial support. These agencies might be either private or public—foundation or business as well as governmental.

3. What the formal channels of getting such support would be.

4. What the informal ways of communicating with those who later might be formally approached are.

5. What kind of support from outside the government or outside a foundation or business firm might help to make government agencies or foundations or business firms feel the idea

worthwhile. In such a case as this, professional support would probably count for much more than public or constituency backing. To be sure, a senator from New York State might respond favorably to a request from Puerto Rican constituents that he endorse the proposal, but it would be highly unlikely that any significant number of Puerto Ricans in New York would vote differently in the next election or even provide more or less in the way of campaign funds because of whatever he did on such an issue. It is not likely to have enough priority. Whereas officials in Health, Education, and Welfare, Foreign Aid administrators, and foundation executives will be continuously concerned with the judgments of university associations, professional groups in social science and the humanities, etc. It might turn out that library facilities would be a key factor with such groups and associations—and that the best way to get their support, or at any rate avoid their opposition, would be to improve libraries at the University of Puerto Rico. Similarly, Foreign Aid administrators, the State Department, and the like will respond partly in terms of their guess as to the way in which Caribbean nations regard Puerto Rico—and it may be the case that the university can do something to affect such guesses. It might show that Puerto Rico is more popular with and admired by Caribbean and Latin American *intellectuals* than it is with Caribbean and Latin American *governments* (some of which have not been enthusiastic about the Popular party social-democratic regime in Puerto Rico). On the other hand, there may be nothing that the University of Puerto Rico can do to affect such guesses, for they may be dependent upon historic, demographic, and cultural factors, quite beyond control.

6. Among those whose favorable support is important after calculations (2) through (5), which are the most likely to be *sympathetic* and therefore provide good starting points and

7. Among those whose favorable support is important after calculations (2) through (5), which are the most *accessible*.

8. Among those whose favorable support is important after calculations (2) through (5), which ones are the most *able to provide really effective support*.

9. Then there is a final calculation—weighing possible sympathy, accessibility, and power against each other, where should the start be made? The temptation is of course to start with the most accessible; but this is often wasteful; they may only be mildly predisposed to sympathy and/or not powerful.

It is worth reporting that, although I spent some weeks in 1961 trying to develop plans for such an institute in Puerto Rico, neither I, nor any of those with whom I worked, as far as I recollect, got beyond mere formal arguments and approaches. Yet, we, because of a background in politics, were more predisposed than most academics to be aware of the need for analyzing influence.

Calculations of the sort just listed help to locate and focus influence; they can help to make latent influence active; *but they can rarely create influence.* This is not to say that it is impossible to create influence. But the creation of influence is more a matter of "public relations" or propaganda than of government relations; it will not be discussed in this book, although there are government relations specialists and Washington representatives who also spend a good deal of time on public relations, propaganda, and political campaigning. But the techniques are different. They have been discussed so frequently elsewhere that there is no occasion to deal with them here.

X.

What has just been said is really this: *The effective Washington representative provides influence for his client by acquiring and translating relevant information.* In this sense, of course, he does "provide influence and information . . ." but this is probably not the sense in which inexperienced clients expect to buy or rent influence. And, in fact, clients often have to be taught that this is what they can in fact get and use.

It is desirable to underline the point that the Washington representative deals with two kinds of information. The first kind is apparent enough—information about the factual and legal aspects of the issues with which his clients are concerned. Second, he supplies relevant information about influence relationships or influence potentialities in a given situation. If, for instance, it is known that a given congressman is in debt because of campaign expenses, it is more likely that he will be particularly responsive to an invitation to address a trade association meeting for a fee. Or, if the most active commissioner of a given regulatory agency is supporting a particular presidential aspirant, to whom victory in a particular state primary is important, representations by lawyers, active in the politics of that particular state, may be especially helpful. Or if a medical or educational officer in the Department of Health, Education, and Welfare, whose support is desired for a certain ruling, is a candidate for the presidency of a given university, a trustee of that university may have better access to and more influence with him than most people.

However, there is a danger which may affect some Washington representatives and clients. Information about these influence relationships can be helpful; in most instances, however, their effect is marginal. Some people are in a sense unduly Machiavellian in viewpoint—they exaggerate the role of power and pull in U.S. governmental decisions, or simply have a passion for the "inside dope," the "real reason." They can and do waste a good deal of time in focusing on influence relationships rather than on the merits of the case—or in trying to cultivate influence of their own through contacts, rather than dealing with the issues. The latter type is dismissed by some sophisticated Washington hands with a phrase about "those guys who think government relations is playing golf out at Burning Tree . . ." (Prominent people supposedly relax at Burning Tree; and are then more susceptible, supposedly, to blandishments from representatives of business firms and other organizations).

On the whole, in Washington, my *impression*—without any hard evidence to support it—is that more Washington representatives pay too *little* explicit attention to the influence factor than pay too *much* attention to it.* My *impression*, also is that the situation is just the reverse in some state capitals.

There is one other approach to information which must be included in a sophisticated government relations program. That is the *intelligence* approach, the approach designed to take account of contingencies which could develop. The careful Washington representative will, for instance, keep track of bills and resolutions which are filed—to see if any of them *might* affect the interests of his organization. Of course, the overwhelming majority of bills and resolutions have nothing to do with his particular organization—but, sometimes, there are unexpected consequences from proposals which do not, at first glance, appear connected. For instance, should representatives of a university or of associations of college professors or students take any stand on a proposal for penalizing travel to Europe in order to protect the balance of payments? Or could the National Parking Association benefit from some proposal to finance training of school dropouts?

Certainly, too, the great majority of bills and resolutions are not going anywhere. They will be filed and that will be the end of them. But, as a measure of protection, it may be desirable to see if there is a sleeper among seemingly hopeless proposals.

Similarly, of course, a sophisticated government relations staff monitors, *within the limits of available time and personnel*, committee reports and hearings which may be relevant.

And, even more important, a sophisticated program involves

---

* This may have changed since 1963.

keeping track of regulations and proposals for regulations which may be relevant to the client's interests.

Of course, no one person can possibly follow, comprehendingly, most of the numerous proposals for bills, investigations, and regulations. There are too many—their implications are too broad. It is for this reason that experience is vital in much Washington representation. For, it is experience, aided by study and imagination, which can enable a person to guess that such-and-such a form of words may well mean that a proposed bill or regulation or investigation might affect his organization's interests. At any rate, the perception of such possible contingent connections is a specific kind of skill, which some persons who know a great deal about government lack.

Of course, in a government relations program of any size, it is not necessary that everyone possess this skill. But it is highly useful in such a program to have someone in its employ who does possess it.

XI.

In any presentation of the sort made in this chapter, it is difficult to steer a straight course between Scylla and Charybdis. On the one hand, there is a tendency to write so as to confirm familiar impressions (in this case that would mean to support the notions which many have derived from newspaper stories about corruption and pull in government). On the other, there is a temptation, in challenging the familiar and conventional impressions, to overstate one's case (or at least to write so that one appears to do so).

Were we starting this discussion with a naive faith in rational democracy, ignorant of the existence of interests and organizations, and of their role in politics and government, no doubt much emphasis would have to be placed upon the role of deals, special access, etcetera, in government and governmental decision-making. But we are not starting out on any such basis; in fact, the literature of lobbying and pressure politics, ever since the days of Mark Hanna and the Populists, has emphasized the role of wheeler-dealers in legislation and administration. Anyone who has, for instance, read Drew Pearson's columns over the years will have learned that deals do happen, influence is exerted, people are paid off, and so forth.

Accordingly, it is not at all necessary to stress these matters. However, in calling attention to the far greater importance of other forms of exerting influence I have probably failed to take enough account of three respects in which pull, very crude deals, and so forth, may work:

a. The "one-shot" operator probably can on occasion help himself a good deal by buying pull—and if he has enough resources, he may be able to pay a high enough price genuinely to buy it. But, in fact, there are not very many one-shot operators. *And in any case this book is written from the standpoint of the organization that is likely to have a continuing relationship with government.* Few one-shot operators would read it or be guided by it. (By a "one-shot" operator, I mean a man who has one very important favor or ruling to get from government and will not need any subsequent concessions of any great importance. An example might be a firm dependent for survival upon a particular land concession, but, which, if granted the land rights, might not need to go again to Washington for ten years.)

b. I have emphasized that what I say applies only to Washington—and not necessarily to states or cities, and still less to certain foreign governments. But there is a great difference in the organizational ethics and climate of different departments and regulatory agencies; I do not pretend to know all of the bureaus in Washington. It is possible, perhaps even probable, that there is some bureau or regulatory commission which practices politics and government in the fashion of some of the states, rather than like other Washington agencies. I am speaking, in other words, about what is characteristic of Washington, not what is necessarily true of every agency, bureau, and section.

I would be speaking out of unsupported suspicions if I were to name current examples as illustrating such exceptions; but it does seem to have been the case that the Alien Property administration just after World War II was more vulnerable to pull and rather crude deals than most agencies. It also seems definitely to have been the case that just prior to World War II the consular service was similarly susceptible; although in this case it might be regarded as more of a "one-shot operation" where persons desiring special favors could and did make very high payments to underpaid officials.

c. It is important to stress that the general freedom of the Washington bureaucracy from susceptibility to illegitimate pull or crude deals is *in part* due to support from the highest executive and congressional officials. (Vice versa, of course, politicians coming to Washington are often more honest and objective than they were in earlier careers in state politics, because the cumulative impact of the Washington bureaucracy, the national press, and the Washington tradition pushes them toward a greater degree of honesty and integrity). During the Harding administration, notably, there were some occasions when top executives connived at or benefited from crudely dishonest deals. There have been a few such instances since; and no doubt any given organization or Washington representative might be dealing with men who similarly violate the Washington tradition in the future. But in dealing with such executives or congressmen, the warnings given in this whole chapter apply. And, in particular (and this is very different from the situation in many state governments) an organization which engages in bribery and corruption of a Washington official of any prominence may well be handicapping itself for years to come; for, in the Washington situation, such bribes and corruption may well be exposed, and, if they are, all those who deal with the bribing organization in the future may well lean over backwards to avoid any suspicion of favoritism towards it.

Of course, in principle, it is possible that the national government as a whole might become genuinely corrupt and come to resemble highway departments, for instance, in such states as Oklahoma, West Virginia, and Indiana, not long ago. The odds against such a development appear to me, however, to be very great; the whole thrust of our times towards bureaucratic accountability and efficiency and professionalism seems to be moving us, as a nation, in the opposite direction. Indeed, a change in this direction in our national government would be as much of a revolution as the New Deal in its time or the Jacksonian introduction of the spoils system in the earlier days of the republic. Not only this book, but much of what is now written about government in Washington, would become outdated should this direction alter.

8

CHARACTERISTIC TENSIONS BETWEEN CLIENTS AND FREE PROFESSIONALS

*Situations Where
Washington Representatives and Their Employers
Irritate Each Other*

The issues raised in this chapter affect government relations specialists and Washington representatives, but also many other professionals: researchers, consultants, lawyers, college professors, artists, photographers, engineers, accountants. So far as I am aware, although there are discussions of the problems of particular professions, there is no general treatment of the basic issue, which is: *What are the characteristic difficulties, inherent in the relationship of free professionals, as such, to their employers or clients?*

The particular problems of government relations specialists

may be better understood in terms of a general approach. Furthermore, most readers of this book have reason to be concerned with this general approach, either because of their own professional experience or because of contact with professionals, hired by organizations with which they are connected.

Consequently, this chapter is a bit different in orientation from the other chapters. I have tried to suggest some of the general problems of free professionals in relationship to their clients. For those whose interest is in the practical problems of Washington representation, that section may be skipped; also some political scientists, concerned chiefly with general politics, may wish to skip the entire chapter. I hope, on the other hand, that it may be of interest to students of the sociology of work and of the professions.

I.

GENERAL.

The term "free professional" refers to an employee or self-employed person who has a considerable "say" in deciding how his job shall be carried out—and who himself tends to determine his own priorities. Archetypal examples of free professionals are distinguished medical specialists, whose practice is entirely private, or well-known novelists.

As the term is used here, a person is a free professional, *not because of any formal contract or relationship*, but because of the way in which he does his job. Take, for illustration, research interviewers on two different projects—one, working full time as an employee at a commercial firm, the other on an intermittent arrangement with a university research center. The university project involves asking specified questions, which must be given exactly, according to the instructions on the schedule; the commercial organization encourages the interviewer to put any questions or make any observations which are congenial to him, so long as they result in findings which are ultimately helpful. In the university case, the interviewer is, then, *not* a free professional; but the commercial employee is one. (The contrasting examples just given really existed; I am thinking of interviewers employed on two different studies of the same organization, one conducted by a university under a foundation grant, the other by a business management firm, under contract to a commercial client).

The classic contrast between a free professional and one who is not is between the self-employed artist, free to choose his own perspective, techniques, and approach, and the "bull pen artist," forced to follow in detail the plans of his employers. Some jobs which once were almost free professions have lost their freedom. Crafts, such as furniture-repairing or even shoe-making,[1] once had some aspects of a free profession. On the other hand, college teaching which in some early denominational colleges, apparently, involved following set lessons and texts, has become increasingly a free profession in practice and principle.

II.

GOVERNMENT RELATIONS AS A FREE PROFESSION.

Washington representation and government relations ought to be free professions. No headquarters can prescribe for the man on the spot how the job should be done. It is impossible for the main office to assess what should be priorities at a given moment, simply because it cannot judge as well as the Washington representative himself what it is practical to achieve. Strict supervision of the government relations program can only be justified in two sorts of circumstances: (1) the chief executive himself may in fact spend a substantial proportion of his time, continuously, on

---

[1] See, for demonstration, the elegant *Autobiography of John Younger, Shoemaker, St. Boswell's* (Kelso, Scotland: J. H. Rutherfurd, 1881).

Washington relations and may know the job better than those who bear the title, or (2) the organization's governmental contacts are extremely limited and specific.

It makes little difference whether the Washington representative is a part-time consultant, on retainer, with a dozen other clients, or a full-time employee, whose sole obligation is to the organization and its interests. In either case, he must have, if he is to do his best for the client, the same kind of freedom as a senior university professor or a psychiatrist.

BUT LACK OF TRUST BETWEEN FREE PROFESSIONAL AND CLIENT IS PARTLY JUSTIFIED

There are many inherent difficulties in the relationship between the free professional, on the one hand, and his client or employer, on the other. The most basic: The client does not really trust the free professional—he feels that the latter is not his agent, is doing something behind his back, is perhaps double-crossing him, letting him down.

This is, I suspect, a likely development as soon as the free professional takes the viewpoint, "I serve your *interests*, not your *desires*." (The quotation is from Edmund Burke in his great speech on representation to the electors of Bristol). For, naturally, the client or employer immediately, at the moment, does not always distinguish between desires and interests; his desires, indeed, he will often regard as his interests. But the professional— whose perspective is broader, who is more apt to think in the long run—does make such a distinction. Frequently, he will be guided by some long-run or complex aspect of a situation which never occurs to the client; that is why, in part, the client employs him. But it is also why, in part, the client mistrusts him. If he is fortunate, he can persuade the client to follow his judgment in detail; but frequently, both for the sake of the client and the sake of his own professional reputation, he must to some extent mislead or obfuscate the client on details. (Of course, on a much larger scale, because the "clients" [the voters] are so much more numerous, often so much less well-informed and more impulsive, and because their desires are so much more amorphous, the skillful politician—the statesman—must also do exactly what Burke said: represent the clients' interests, not their desires, and so incur their suspicion).

Similarly, the lawyer will try to get the client to reach an accommodation with a plaintiff, or to "cop a plea"—or the psychiatrist, consulting the patient's future *interests*, as he sees them, and not his present *demands*, will attempt to lead him into doing something he does not want to do.

The lack of trust between client and professional is not, however, due just to the client's failure to perceive his own interests. On the contrary, once any employee is free to choose his own way of proceeding, there is always a chance that he may take advantage of an employer. For instance, take the following cases: Is the client fairly treated or not?

Item: A Washington representative of a "cause" group believes that a certain member of Congress is an unusually valuable congressman. This member never has done and is unlikely to do anything for the particular cause. Nevertheless, the Washington representative uses the money-raising list of the organization to get campaign funds for the congressman; and he furthermore recruits volunteer workers for the congressman in the latter's home district, through the organization. To be sure, the friendship thus enhanced, may mean that on matters of indifference, the congressman might do something for the Washington representative, but there are other members, sympathetic to the cause, who would do more.

Item: A Washington representative has a personal friend whose son wants an appointment as a congressional page. He uses the entree given him by his organizational position to get the boy the job.

Item: A Washington representative of a church group, which is much concerned about international relations and race, is himself personally more concerned with problems of pollution and "environmental defense." He manages to smuggle into an annual resolution of the church a statement which authorizes action in this line—and he then spends 25 or 30 percent of his time on pollution-control legislation. Probably, some members of Congress think his denomination actually cares about the matter; at any rate, he deprives the denomination of time which its leaders budgeted for other purposes.

Item: A Washington representative of a trade union is an old-line believer in free trade. His national board, responding to the requests and warnings of the industry has ordered him to support quota and restrictive provisions, along with the trade association. However, he himself is close to other big international unions, takes his cue from general AFL-CIO policy, and supports reciprocal trade—going to the extent of arguing with protectionist congressmen that the industry whose employees he represents and plants of which are in their districts would not be hurt by more liberal trade. He is, of course, taking the stand that he is advocating the *interests* of the workers, even if not their *desires*. He probably would defend himself further by saying that if the national board had seriously cared they could have found out what he was doing.

Item: Somewhat the reverse of the above, there is a national board supporting a liberal trade position, and a Washington representative whose own craft background had been in a small and dying segment of the industry, which is hurt by foreign imports. He frequently tells congressmen and other leaders of the ill-effects of foreign imports.

Any one of these situations certainly could make a client suspicious. Yet, any one of them could be, to some extent, justified as having long-range advantages to the client organization. It is perhaps illuminating to suggest that they are similar to problems that arise in other free professions: a doctor prescribes expensive brand-name drugs for his patients, made by a company in which he owns stock, but he bought stock in that company because he respects its meticulous care in manufacturing; a teacher uses his student assistants to run personal errands for him, but justifies this because it saves his time for teaching and research; a research associate diverges sharply from the research design set out by his chief, but answers questions of more importance from his stand-point; a lawyer arranges with the district attorney to "cop a plea" for a particular client, less advantageous than the client could have got, but in return the lawyer is able to make better arrange-ments for *other* clients; an architect persuades a client to approve a design far more expensive than the latter needs or can afford, but it is exceptionally beautiful! etc, etc, etc.

III.

THE WASHINGTON REPRESENTATIVE IS UNDER A DISADVANTAGE BECAUSE OF HIS CONTACT WITH THE OUTSIDER, "THE ENEMY."

As far as the preceding goes, Washington representatives do not differ from any other free professionals. Some of them do in fact exploit clients; and many are thought to be doing so, when they are in fact serving interests, rather than desires.

But a Washington representative is under one additional disadvantage, which has already been mentioned. The very nature of his job forces him—if he is honest and responsible—to try to interpret opposing viewpoints to the client. A pharma-ceutical sales manager may be assigned to government relations. After awhile, he will begin to see (a) that there is more to the Kefauver-Humphrey-Fountain position on regulation of pharma-ceuticals than he had thought, or (b) at least that a great many responsible people take the Kefauver-Humphrey-Fountain case seriously. And he will see that his organization *must* understand (b) and perhaps should understand (a). But in trying to in-terpret (b) and possibly (a) he will put himself in a position of sounding disloyal. His former colleagues will be annoyed and irritated; and they will therefore be more censorious of any way in which he appears to take advantage of his job than they were when he was in sales management. For instance, if he gets interested in the anti-poverty program and possible participation of the firm in it, and goes ahead to look into such matters, they may murmur about exploitation. Whereas, when he was simply in sales in some regional office, and spent firm time on a service-club project for fatherless boys, everybody condoned or even applauded it.

Anyone who goes from some other branch of an organization to government relations or Washington representation should be aware that he may well be exposed to criticism of this type for the reason just suggested. And although he may be saddened by losing his rapport with his old colleagues, he should realize that it is part of the job; he can no more be one with them, now that he is in the government relations slot, than he could be had he been made chief executive of the entire firm. People in either of these posts get a different perspective and are likely to be regarded as betraying old colleagues.

A Washington representative who comes from outside an organization or industry will not meet quite these problems of social-psychological adjustment. But he will also be suspect—he "isn't really one" of the organization; he will be regarded as being too much of a Washington type. His natural—and possibly correct—reaction is to interpret all this as showing the naiveté of clients. But it is well to try to temper such an interpretation with the attitude, "were I in their position, I would feel as they do."

THE WASHINGTON REPRESENTATIVE IS LIKELY TO BE THE MAN IN THE MIDDLE.

In relationship to some agencies, a Washington representative who has a background in government, particularly with the agency, and then represents an interest group, suffers much the same difficulty as our hypothetical pharmaceutical salesman who went to Washington. His former colleagues in government may feel he has "sold out." I suppose that I have heard at least fifty sneering references, involving such imputations, to people who have had some governmental or quasi-governmental experience and are now working for an interest group.[2]

And often, of course, government agencies, and still more, good-will cause groups or professional organizations regard the representatives of private interests, no matter what their background, as conservative, hidebound, reactionary, and benighted. So, the very Washington representative who is not trusted by the organization which employs him because he is not whole-hearted enough in its cause, may be regarded as stupidly dedicated to it by others to whom he tries to present its case. "You can't win" in a sense; the Washington representative must, in many instances, necessarily be a man in the middle—and at a disadvantage because the people on either side of him have no idea how far the other side goes. I had a recent example of this: talking with officers of a big, rather conservative, professional association, I referred to the representative of a given interest group as "liberal." "Oh, no," they said immediately "quite conservative . . . almost reactionary. . . ." The point was that they

---

[2] An extreme, but interesting, example of this. In working on *American Business and Public Policy* (New York: Atherton, 1963), which was a study of reciprocal trade legislation, I naturally tried to take a fair viewpoint towards the opponents of extended trade, and to overcome the prejudice in favor of liberal trade which is generally part of an academic background. (As one of the leading protectionist congressmen said to me, "In my district, the only people against me on this are the college professors and those women [League of Women Voters]." An old line labor leader, heartwarmingly sincere, explained to me that college professors favor free trade because they are against the poor workingman). My explanation of how I tried to do this provoked some violent comments from former friends and associates. Two thoroughly acrimonious letters were inspired by this circumstance in reaction to my "Representative and His District," Reprint PS-63 (Indianapolis: Bobbs-Merrill) and my "Role Relationships and Conceptions of Neutrality in Interviewing," *American Journal of Sociology*, 63 (1956), 153–157.

were familiar with the man in the Washington milieu; whereas
I had heard about him from people in his industry.

IV.

One of the most serious sources of difficulties in the Washington
representative relationship—as with many other free professions
—is that the client's *real* purposes may be different from his
expressed ones. A good many patients, it is said, go to doctors in
order to have somebody listen to them. They do not really wish
advice about improving their health.

Similarly, some clients employ Washington representatives
in order to enhance their own personal prestige. They want to
feel they have a pipeline to some "inside dope"; they want to
meet famous people. In such cases, a Washington representative
who tries to do a job which is best for the organization taken as
a whole will prove irritating. Perhaps few chief executives of
business firms will say outright, "What I want is to have the
Vice-President stay with me when he visits our city. . . ," but
a perceptive Washington representative can usually guess that
this sort of thing is the client's main interest. After all, a good
many men, by the time they have become chief executives of an
organization, are looking about for some new extra-organizational
source of prestige. Perhaps they want mere social prominence.
Perhaps they want to serve on prestigious national commissions.

If they make this clear to the Washington representative in
advance, he is free to accept or reject the bargain. But, in many
cases, the Washington representative will *ostensibly* be hired for
something else—in some instances which might be cited except
that there is no way of doing so discreetly, something like this
happens: In all good faith, the Washington representative ac-
cepts an offer to serve an organization and its purposes. The chief
executive or the top staff do not make clear that, in reality, it
is their personal objectives rather than those of the organization

on which the representative is to concentrate. In some instances, perhaps they have not themselves articulated their hopes; in others, they would not wish to formulate them, and expect the representative to be shrewd enough to know what is really desired. Now, a representative who is conscientious and cautious—especially one recruited from the Washington bureaucracy, without much experience in legal practice or local politics—may lack such shrewdness. Or he may feel that there is an ethical issue involved.

Obviously, such situations create tensions. A Washington representative of a state government might, for instance, be expected to promote the Presidential or Cabinet aspirations of a governor, if he is directly responsible to the latter. Probably without any qualms of conscience, he can (if skillful enough) arrange for his top executives to get national publicity. But should he devote a good deal of his time, if employed by a good-will organization or a business firm, in trying to settle the tax problems of the chief executives in their private capacities? Should he, if employed by a business firm, devote most of his time to some cause in which the chief executives are interested, and of no concern to the stockholders: impeaching Earl Warren or conserving some national forest?

No blanket solution, probably, can be applied here but any Washington representative ought to realize that he may at any time meet such issues and know how to deal with them. Indeed, some years ago the National Association of Trade Association executives put on a skit, with a series of dilemmas for the Washington-based executive. Most of them involved personal services to important people in the client organization, and the purpose was to get the trade association executives to reflect about what to do under such circumstances. The discussion suggested that there was nothing unfamiliar in the dilemmas posed. (What, for instance, should a Washington representative do about getting the son of the head of a good-will organization for which he works into Annapolis or West Point? How much time should he spend on getting an invitation to a highly restricted social event for a board member who is not the chief executive?)

V.

Another difficulty may be conflict in the client or employing organization. This may be obvious in state governments: the governor may be all out to get funds for some particular Federally-financed project, which the legislature will oppose. In such an instance the Washington representative will know who hired him and to whom he must be loyal. In business firms, or trade associations, it is often harder to get a clear picture of the patterns of conflict. Some Washington representatives, hired from outside an industry, have overcommitted and embarrassed themselves because they did not realize that the top executives did not have support throughout the organization. Vice versa, there has been a tendency in government agencies and even, occasionally, in Congress, to assume that a Washington representative speaks for a larger segment of his organization than is in fact the case.

VI.

Clients need to be aware that Washington representatives who come from outside their own organization have a career-pattern and loyalties of their own. A good many economists, for instance, in Washington, will be influenced more by their feeling about what other economists regard as respectable as by the needs of their client or his long-term interests. I have seen newspapermen, turned Washington representatives, reject out of hand what may have been a worthwhile suggestion for publicizing a proposal of their organization's, simply because they could not stomach the idea of being made fun of by their ex-colleagues.

Some Washington representatives, taken from the bureaucracy, naturally and usefully, keep up contacts with those in their old shop. But, for this very reason, they are sensitive to the opinions of the latter and this sensitivity may prevent them from going as far as they might in their client's best interests. And a good many Washington representatives, who used to work on Capitol Hill, hope or expect to go back there some day—perhaps with a senator or committee clerk whose help they are now seeking. So they do not press very hard.

Human nature being what it is, people are not necessarily going to admit the influence of such reference groups and expectations upon them. They will have good-sounding reasons for doing something accommodating. Frequently these reasons will be defensible, but sometimes they are cover-ups.

There is no simple solution to such matters. But a client who is sensitive to his Washington representative's ambitions, social contacts, and reference groups may be able to suspect when his "reasons" are merely excuses to avoid embarrassment with former or future colleagues. And a Washington representative who is conscious of his own motivations may be able to handle them more intelligently than if he is not. No doubt, this would not help the client in the case where the man expected to go back to Capitol Hill; the Washington representative would, aware or not, pull his punches there. But, in the case of the newspapermen mentioned above, they simply were not conscious of the "audience" they had in mind, and if they had weighed rationally the value to their client of the proposal, against the possibility of being laughed at by former colleagues for a day or two, they would probably have done a better job for the client.[3]

[3] See the discussion of "the imagined audience" in several articles in L. Dexter and D. White, *People, Society, and Mass Communications* (New York: Free Press, 1964), especially an article by Raymond A. Bauer, pp. 125-140.

VII.

There are a number of other issues to which there is no simple solution but where awareness on both sides may help. For instance, Washington representatives, properly, cooperate with representatives of other groups and organizations. Inevitably, cooperation sometimes leads to taking part in something of no great moment to a particular client. Sometimes, this may be a perfectly rational return of favors or an effort to increase the likelihood of future favors. But, in other cases, it may be simply that the Washington representative, having worked with other men for awhile, does not like to say "No, we cannot go along on this . . ." but, if he did say "No," it would spare time and resources for something more valuable to his client.

VIII.

All these issues cut across one other of considerable importance. The Washington representative, in contact with a wide range of public concerns and issues, is apt to feel that he has a broader conception of public interest and of the client's long-term interests than has the client himself. He may let such a concern lead him into issues which raise such questions as this: Should a representative of a business firm be concerned with proposals for avoiding riots in the cities? Should a trade union Washington representative involve himself in pollution controls?

Any such activity by a Washington representative involves risks; some people in the organization will fail to see the relevance or will strongly oppose a particular program which he supports. There is no easy answer here. To the extent that a man is fully professional, he should be encouraged to spend some time on such broad matters. Such a viewpoint fits into the general conception of government relations programs as developing broader representation, discussed in the next chapter.

But the temptation to attempt too much and the temptation, also, to neglect the client's major concerns, both are dangers if clients let representatives concern themselves with general government, in this sense.

Perhaps, the best solution would be, where clients are so inclined, to specify that Washington representatives may spend up to 20 percent of their time on general matters, and that they should limit the number of such general matters to which they address themselves to two or three—so as to really accomplish something, rather than to just make statements.

9

THE BASIC PUBLIC SERVICE OF GOVERNMENT RELATIONS PROGRAMS

Interpretation . . . Stability . . . Towards a Wider System of Representation in Politics

Members of a profession ought to have a formulation of their highest public service, of their fundamental contribution to society. Doctors help achieve health and avoid pain; lawyers contribute to justice and promote order. Teachers, at their best, spread enlightenment. There is not as yet any such general conception of mission in the government relations field.

Washington representatives do interpret diverse viewpoints and in so doing contribute to social stability. They also broaden the representative process in our society.

INTERPRETATION.

If we had some kind of measure of the cumulative effect of lobbying and Washington representation—if we knew how to weigh precisely the question "What difference does it all make?" —we would find that the biggest effect of Washington representation has been *not* on Washington but on clients. For, in the nature of the case, Washington representatives and government relations staffs have, constantly, to be explaining and interpreting (a) legislation (b) regulations (c) the reasons for legislation and regulations (d) viewpoints of opposing, conflicting interests (e) to some extent, why these latter have such viewpoints. In so doing, they sometimes suggest, consciously or unconsciously, modifications of the prevailing viewpoint in their own organization. Undoubtedly, in ninety-nine cases out of a hundred, what they write and what they say gets far more attention in their own organization than from anybody in Washington.

It is worth noting, too, that even in formulating statements of their organization's policy, they modify and interpret. Because, frequently enough, the Washington staff takes a draft by the chief executive or his associates and says, "Yes, but . . . we've got to remember, this is what the Bureau thinks . . . and though you are right, still we have to take account of that . . . ," and "there's no point in getting the union's hackles up by saying this because. . . ."

STABILITY.

The total effect of these interpretations has been to increase the orderliness of our society. In the 1930's, a good many business executives felt as violently about Washington and what it did to them as Black Power types do now. At other times, other interests have had similar reactions. But business, especially, and others too, have been influenced over the last thirty years by an ever increasing number of interpreters, that is to say Washington representatives.

"Consensus" is regarded as a desirable political objective. Washington representation contributes interpretations which lead towards consensus. Increasingly, interest groups in our society, faced with a problem with government, hire somebody who, in fact, spends a great deal of his time teaching them what government wants, why it wants it, and what the opposing interests are and why they have to be taken account of.

And such interpretations diminish the likelihood that anybody will feel he has to go outside the system. Rather, failure leads to the feeling "We had better accommodate ourselves to these realities . . ." (a very different response from that of many businessmen to the New Deal), or else "we had better sharpen our tools of interpretation."

Just at present there are two—possibly three—groups which might seriously be expected to resort to violence. These are the urban poor, especially the Negro poor,[1] the Southern poor whites, and possibly a minority of students. The Negro poor—as distinguished from the Negro middle-class—have had little representation in Washington. Neither have Southern poor whites. And students, due to reasons of age, and other factors in our society, have very little representation in Washington.[2]

There is a fourth possible source of violent resistance to government—the Vietnam War. And this is, as pointed out earlier, a case where interpretation in the characteristic Washington sense has failed, or come close to failing. But there is still some successful interpretation.

There are many other interests and groups which have been

---

[1] It is true that the Negro-poor will probably be led by middle-class Negroes; but these will be mostly young student-type radicals.

[2] For some background factors on student orientations see Lewis Dexter, *Tyranny of Schooling* (New York: Basic Books, 1964).

deprived or aggrieved over the last thirty years. Their leaders, however, have been influenced by the interpretations of their own Washington representatives—not people hired by somebody else, but people on their own pay-roll, interpreting in their own language. So, they do not contemplate violence.

Of course, this is merely to say that Washington representatives are *one* factor in social stability. It would be foolish to say they are *the* cause of stability, and of the related, rather high degree of tolerance found in contemporary American group conflict. So, also, it would be foolish to say that lawyers and our legal system are the bases for the kind of order we have in the United States or Canada. But, just as lawyers contribute considerably to this order—just as the legal system is a necessary, even if not a sufficient, condition for orderly living in our times— so Washington representation and active government relations programs are a necessary,[3] even if not a complete, basis for stability in modern life.

A BROADENING SYSTEM OF REPRESENTATION.

The third great contribution of Washington representatives and government relations is to enlarge the whole area of representation. With rare exceptions people who have a case can be heard *and are heard* in Washington. And most people who have a cause or a grievance, learn that this is true, that there is indeed a chance to be heard. (The sadness of the "Black Power" movement is that its leaders have not learned this—because, of course, for so many years Negroes were not heard in Washington; their descendents do not see that times have changed.)

Now, in Congress, there are a few hundred members, elected on a one-man, one-vote basis, from districts where the social

---

[3] No doubt, some equivalent could be invented; but in practice, government relations programs are basic to what we have.

structure is quite similar. Consequently, it is arithmetically impossible that there should be members in any given Congress who attach *priority* to most causes and concerns. There may be members who sympathize; there may be members who will vote "right"; there may be members who will hold committee hearings, if given backing. But it is sheer accident, if, year in and year out, there is a congressman who deeply concerns himself, for instance, with the interests of the American Indians, or of the people who believe in natural nutrition, or of the chiropractors, or, for that matter, of such medium-sized industries as paper-manufacturing or musical instruments, or of such professions as the teaching of the handicapped, or girls' physical education.

Yet, through government relations programs, and Washington representation, there are people in Washington who speak for many of these interests, year in and year out, and do attach great priority to them. If the executive branch is against a concern as it is in the case of chiropractic or natural nutrition, these people can and do keep the cause alive. They make its followers feel there is still a chance within the system; and that feeling is correct.

In the complex, diversified modern world with its rapid communications, representation through Congress is not enough. The Washington representative provides an additional valuable type of representation, one which congressmen with their more general constituencies cannot furnish. This is not to say that Washington representatives are, usually, rivals to congressmen; rather, they supplement what congressmen do.

In some cases, Washington representatives supplement Congress, not only by speaking for organizations and causes but by providing a supplementary method of what is really legislation. There have been cases where members of a legislative committee have in effect said to representatives of conflicting interests: "You get together and work out a bill. We will probably accept what you agree on." There have been other cases where Washington representatives of different groups, gathered in a coalition, have hammered out a set of proposals, which have served as a basis for the final legislative product—and, within the coalition, there has been the same sort of mutual accommodation and trading which takes place in a legislative committee. And when Congress allows power to regulate to the executive branch, the relevant executive agency will sometimes start by finding out what is acceptable to affected interests. And the affected interests often speak through their Washington representatives—so that legislative delegation is not only to the executive branch *but to the affected interests, through their Washington representatives.*

Assuming the survival in general of the social and governmental system which we now have, such tendencies will probably develop and increase. So, it is a reasonable expectation that Washington representatives will become a more important part of the political system, as the years go by.